Contents

Contents (cont.)

COOPERATIVE LEARNING: SCIENCE

ACTIVITIES,
EXPERIMENTS,
& GAMES

BY ESTHER WEINER

SCHOLASTIC
PROFESSIONAL BOOKS

New York · Toronto · London · Auckland · Sydney

Dedication

I thank my husband, Howard,
my children, Jonathan and Michael,
and my parents and sisters,
whose enthusiasm gave
me the courage
to write another book.

I thank the administration and staff
of E.M. Baker School in Great Neck,
New York, for providing endless
opportunities for exploration, both
in science and in the science and art
of teaching.

Designed by Nancy Metcalf
Production by Intergraphics
Cover design by Vincent Ceci
Cover illustration by Mona Mark
Illustrations by Joe and Terri Chicko, Nancy Metcalf

ISBN 0-590-49240-3

Introduction: Integrating Cooperative Learning with "Whole Science"

These days, educators are finding that cooperative learning and whole language offer many advantages in dealing with the crowded curriculum they must teach.

Although I am a teaching Science Consultant and do not deal directly with other curriculum areas, I have found that children are more successful with science when it is dealt with in a whole language way. In this book, therefore, I offer suggestions to help you easily integrate science with other learning areas, so that you can "crunch" curriculum time effectively and also give your students varied approaches toward understanding the science concepts underlying the activities.

The hands-on science lessons include a section entitled Connections. This suggests ways to integrate the science principles covered in a lesson into math, social studies, language arts, and art, as well as other areas of science. Expository writing skills are emphasized in almost every lesson, as your students are asked to write hypotheses and to complete observations and conclusions. In other words, if you cannot hook your children directly into a love of science, you can hook them by using a curriculum area in which they are already successful.

Both whole language and cooperative learning emphasize building upon children's life experiences to help them understand new learning situations. When I ask my students to hypothesize, I always encourage them to recall those experiences in everyday life which they might relate to each other to help formulate a hypothesis. Most children, for instance, have had many experiences with Legos and building blocks. Capitalizing upon this, you will find it much easier to help students visualize the activity of particles far too small to be seen if they can think of atoms and molecules as the tiny building blocks of their entire world!

Working cooperatively further empowers children to share their experiences in nonthreatening small groups. When working on a hypothesis, each child is expected to state if he/she agrees or disagrees with the others, and explain why. This activity encourages the growth of good listening skills. Cooperative small group activities also generate more data, making conclusions more valid for each experimental activity.

Specific cooperative learning methods are dealt with in more detail in the section which directly follows this introduction and in each lesson's Cooperative Group Management section.

All of the lessons have a Science Concepts section. As you browse through, you may notice that many of the same concepts recur with very different physical phenomena. All this means is that science itself really is Whole Science. If your children can understand only a few basic science concepts, they will have a key to understanding that "everything is connected to everything" and that the scientific laws which govern our planet also govern the rest of the universe.

Whole Science and a "dirt cheap" approach dovetail beautifully as well, in this day and age of short education dollars. (My previous book of science activities, *Dirt Cheap Science,* may be used in conjunction with this one.) I find it is better to not use fancy scientific equipment to teach concepts elementary students should master. Using everyday found and borrowed objects brings your science down to earth and further empowers your children to understand that the concepts they are learning really do relate to their toys and homes and the nature that surrounds them.

Finally, please expect to have some of your experiments not go exactly as planned, due to bad weather or other conditions beyond your control. Part of the fun of science teaching is the unexpected. Take advantage of these occasions by asking the children to help you brainstorm what went wrong.

What I love about my work is discovering "why things are the way they are" along with my students. I hope you feel the same joy and satisfaction too, when you work with yours!

Note: Unless stated otherwise, all lessons are appropriate for Grades 2 through 5.

If your sessions are flexible in length, you will find that some lessons may fit more comfortably into 45 or 50 minutes than 40 minutes, as the introductory note to these lessons indicates. If your sessions are not flexible, you may find it helpful to streamline the preparation time in these lessons.

Except for the games activities, all of the lessons contain the following sections: Science Concepts, Why Teach This?, Cooperative Group Management, Materials Needed, Getting Started, Procedure, and Connections. The games include Science Skills instead of Concepts, and in most cases cooperative group management forms part of the game rules.

Some lessons have followup activities. Unless otherwise stated, the materials needed and procedure are included in the followup sheets, so that you can assign them as homework if you wish.

Working with Cooperative Learning and Hands-On Science

Why Use Cooperative Learning?

As a science consultant, I have found that combining hands-on science activities with cooperative learning enhances the learning experience both for my students and for myself.

Cooperative learning empowers children with the ability to work with their peers, sharing knowledge and respect for each other's contributions. Individual accountability is by no means diminished but becomes even more important because each cooperative group member is now vital to the group's success. For the same reason, the children's self-esteem is enhanced as well.

Cognitive thinking skills often reach a higher level with small groups because these offer the opportunity for children to analyze, synthesize, and self-evaluate during discussion periods. Cooperative learning enhances children's listening and verbal skills, their sense of belonging to a positive peer group, their reliability, trustworthiness and sense of responsibility, along with other social skills vital to success in adult life.

The opportunity to learn how to function successfully within a group enhances a student's chances of success in the working world. Any job or career requires the ability to cooperate with co-workers, clients, and others.

Where Do I, the Teacher, Fit In and Gain From Cooperative Learning?

As the teacher, your function is to act as a facilitator, supplying feedback on how the groups are functioning, suggesting or modeling appropriate social skills each group needs, and teaching new or remedial skills when appropriate for each group.

You gain the freedom to *not* be a policeperson, trying to keep everyone interested and on task. When children have more of an opportunity to contribute their ideas, and feel that their opinions, even if divergent, are valued, they are more likely to both enjoy and stay focused on the task at hand.

What Size Cooperative Learning Groups Should I Use?

Each lesson suggests a number of children ranging from two to four. In general, the younger the children, the smaller your groups should be. However, in acknowledgement of today's educational economic difficulties, and the difficulties of obtaining and setting up hands-on materials, I would suggest setting up for groups no smaller than four for material sharing, and dividing those groups of four into two partnerships which work loosely together at the table.

How Can I Get Started?

The fastest way to get started is to arrange the furniture in your room so children sit in groups of four, or can move their desks quickly to form groups of four for the science period.

I used a permanent marker to write the numbers 1 through 4 at each seating place. This allows me to use the easy cooperative learning technique which I call "Representative Sharing" and Spencer Kagan calls "Numbered Heads Together" (see the next section).

What Are Some Cooperative Learning Techniques That Function Well with the Lessons In This Book?

First of all, you will need a signal the children respond to immediately with undivided attention. I find that raising my hand, and having the children raise their hands as soon as they see my hand or any other hand up, is enough to quiet the room and stop whatever activity is going on.

After the hands are up, and all is quiet, announce the cooperative learning structure you wish the children to follow.

1. **Partner Sharing:** The children share their reasons for their hypothesis, their observations, and evidence for their conclusions with their partner, who is sitting right next to them.

2. **Group Sharing:** After the Partner Sharing, each set of partners shares with the partners opposite them at their table.

   Partner and Group Sharing are the main techniques I use for enabling each child to stay on task more easily and to feel that everyone's contribution is important to the discussion. Partner and Group Sharing allow children to share their life experiences connected to the data sheet's stated problem while hypothesizing about it.

3. **Representative Sharing:** After all children in the group share their thoughts, the teacher calls out a number from 1 through 4.

   Each child in the group who is sitting at that number rises to report on the group's findings. The teacher selects one of the children standing to report. If the other children standing agree with the representative's report, they sit down to avoid repetition. (To encourage the children, and help them avoid feeling cheated out of reporting, I always compliment those who sit down because they allow us to get along with our experiment without wasting time.)

   This method is particularly good for gathering observations so that the children will have more valid evidence for forming and checking their conclusions. It is also excellent for increasing listening skills.

4. **Dipsticking:** While Dipsticking *per se* is not a cooperative learning technique, it does enable the teacher to check for understanding quickly, and it allows for divergent views in hypotheses, observations, and conclusions to be addressed quickly. When I ask for an "agree or disagree" on a child's response by a showing of thumbs up or down, I can ask any child who has a thumb down to explain why she does not agree. This enables me either to correct any misconceptions or compliment the child who is brave enough to disagree and can back up the divergent view with good evidence.

   Dipsticking is a terrific way to raise the level of participation in a whole class lesson and thus increase the children's attention to the task at hand.

What Division of Labor Should I Use For the Groups?

1. **For Setting Up Science Lessons:** If you are a classroom teacher and not a specialist in science, it is extremely difficult to set up hands-on lessons for a whole class. Invest in a set of trays or sturdy low-sided boxes so you have one for each cooperative group. In the morning, or during your prep, set up a model tray which includes all the equipment needed for a group, placed in the way you feel would work best for the experiment.

   Each week, a different numbered child in each group would be in charge of setting up the group tray, and would be responsible for returning to your stock of materials for any additions or replacements.

2. **For Cleanup:** Each child in the group is responsible for handling equipment with respect and replacing it on the tray. However, the week that child #1 is the Setter, child #2 would be responsible for removing the tray from the table, dismantling the tray, and placing the equipment back into the proper place in the classroom.

3. **Secretary:** The data sheets in this book were created with the idea of providing expository writing practice, a skill which all second through fifth graders can certainly benefit from, so my personal feeling is that each child should be responsible for entering information onto his own data sheet. Another reason I argue against the use of group secretaries is that the data sheets can provide information for everyone in the group to look back upon for subsequent lessons.

   Each group member should be responsible for maintaining a science section or folder and for sharing information with an absentee group member.

   This does not mean there is no place for a secretary during science cooperative learning periods. If an informal discussion of prior group knowledge is taking place, or a group concept or word map is being created, you may wish to have the children appoint a secretary to record each group of four's responses.

4. **Timer, Artist, Cutter, Labeler:** When the lessons call for these jobs, allow the children to select who should have which job but make appropriate suggestions. For instance, if you have children who speak English as a second language and are not yet proficient, you might suggest that they would function well as artists.

How Can I Assess Academic Skills?

This is the area in cooperative learning which probably engenders the most controversy. Should group grades be given? Should children be given individual grades?

Assessment is another strong reason for every child to have the responsibility of producing her own data sheet and maintaining a folder which has data sheets in proper order. You can easily tell that a child understood the activity if the hypothesis, observations, and conclusions are logically written in his own words. For this reason, be sure to inform the children that even if there is agreement within a group about a hypothesis, for instance, they must state their hypothesis in their own words. A folder or portfolio which is arranged chronologically can show trends in academic growth and quality of work.

I feel very strongly that a child's academic grade should not hinge upon the academic performance of their group. Therefore I always mark the data sheets as individual efforts with objective comments, rather than numerical or letter grades.

I also believe that a "quality" or "effort" grade should be given to let the child know that effort is always appreciated and admired, even if an answer happens to be incorrect. I place a letter grade from A through F in the lower right hand corner of the data sheet to indicate my assessment of work quality.

Student self-assessment of individual performance is just as important as teacher assessment, so I always ask my students to grade their effort in the activity by placing a letter grade from A to F in the lower left hand corner.

If there is substantial disagreement about the grade, I meet with the student to discuss our definitions of effort or quality.

How Should Social Skills Be Assessed?

I provide a minute or two at the end of each science session for the group to evaluate themselves on how they functioned as a social group. Some skills to look for include: active listening and integration of ideas during brainstorming sessions, sharing of clearly expressed ideas, constructive criticism of ideas and not of the people expressing the ideas, and following classroom rules which show respect for persons and property.

Some key questions to help the groups evaluate their functioning might include:
• Did they have trouble finishing the activity due to arguing?
• Did they share materials and ideas without friction?
• What can they do to make next week's session go more smoothly?
• Did each child compliment a group member about a specific action or thought shared during the period? (At the beginning of the school year I model several compliments which specifically address behaviors I want reinforced.)

Remember, your function as the teacher is to be constantly circulating and observing group interactions, so you can offer suggestions for problem solving.

How Should Uncooperative Students Be Dealt With?

A time-out table should be available for students who cannot function reasonably well within the group, after you have given them a verbal warning.

Once at the time-out table, the student should evaluate his/her group behavior by filling out a Time-Out Sheet (see the sample on page 109.) This would ask the student to note the activity the group was participating in, the behavior the student engaged in that resulted in visiting the time-out table, and a plan of action which will avoid a recurrence of the incident.

Meet with the student in private to discuss the time-out sheet, so she does not have to "face you down" in front of the group. Be sure to ask the student what you can do to help the situation.

If problems persist, enlist the group's help in dealing with the student by asking them what they might do to help avoid the problem. Compliment both the student and the group every time they demonstrate an improvement in social interaction.

If problems still persist, confer with the student's parents and any support staff in your school who deal with behavioral problems.

If all else fails, you may have to remove the child from the group and have the child work individually. Try to avoid reshuffling the child to another group because this will only send a message to the children that if they don't enjoy working with a particular group, they can force a change by acting up.

How Do I Deal with Other Problems Such As Shyness, Language Difficulties, and Different Ability Levels Within Groups?

There will be few if any academic problems if you have groups which are carefully mixed. Try to put a "spark" into each group, and spread out your more deliberate learners. If your more able students know that they are being graded individually, they will not be fearful that their grades will suffer if they are grouped with someone less academically proficient.

If you use Dipsticking frequently, along with Partner Sharing, your "sparks" will get more satisfaction out of class because they will have an increased amount of time for sharing their views without frantic handwaving. Your more deliberate learners will not be shut out of participation because you will not be calling upon hand-waving "sparks" more than the "deliberators."

If you have children who are not yet proficient in English, be sure they are with other children who might function as interpreters or explainers. Since I have implemented cooperative learning techniques such as Representative Sharing, I have found that the participation level of ESL children has increased greatly. When their number is called, they stand and repeat what their group says to them. The feeling of pride in being able to verbally participate is written all over their faces. The group that these children belong to also develops a feeling of pride, knowing that they have helped this child participate.

Shy children benefit from small groups because they do not have to put themselves "on the line" in front of everyone, they gain confidence within their small group, and they report to the entire class only during Representative Sharing time, when they offer a group opinion or agreed upon answers rather than their own.

How Can I Reinforce Cooperative and Academic Achievement?

I have found that presenting a certificate to reward effort in academic achievement combined with cooperative group behavior is a wonderful reinforcer of desirable student qualities. At the period's end, I present the certificate to these children in front of the rest of the class. I try to catch as many children showing social and academic effort as possible. Note that I do not look for academic achievement based upon correct answers only, but for academic effort. This allows all children to have an equal chance of succeeding.

If a child is unfortunate enough to have been placed in a group which is not functioning cohesively, but he is making an effort to cooperate, I will reward that individual, even though the group did not perform as desired. I do not want children to feel that they have to suffer consequences they did not "earn." There is no faster way to turn children off group work than to penalize them for peer behavior that they cannot control.

At the end of the year, any child who has received and saved 25 certificates can show them to me and receive a High Honors Science Award. I never replace lost certificates, because I feel that it is the student's responsibility to take care of important possessions.

The collecting of certificates allows the children to keep track of their positive behaviors, further reinforcing these behaviors and creating a more positive classroom atmosphere.

I have included some samples of certificates you can use for reinforcement of these desired behaviors. (See page 109 and 110.)

Where Do I Find Out More About Cooperative Learning?

Several cooperative learning schemes have been developed and can be used with all curriculum areas. Spencer Kagan, the Director of Resources of Teachers, 27134 Paseo Espada, #202, San Juan, Capistrano, CA 92675, is an excellent source for courses and readings on cooperative learning.

For a quick overview, see *Cooperative Learning—Getting Started* by Susan S. Ellis and Susan F. Whalen, Scholastic, 1990. Several books by D.W. Johnson offer in-depth analysis of the theory and application of cooperative learning strategies. *Control Theory in the Classroom* by Dr. William Glasser provides a strong argument for using cooperative learning in the classroom to increase the amount of responsibility that students have for their own actions.

COOPERATIVE LEARNING: SCIENCE

Bubbling Molecules

A 40-minute lesson will have your students begging to continue when their investigation of bubbles leads to these . . .

 **Science Concepts**

1. Air is matter and takes up room.
2. Molecules which are alike can attract each other; molecules which are not alike can attract each other even more strongly.

Why Teach This?

All matter is composed of invisible particles called atoms which are usually joined together to form molecules. Water molecules consist of two hydrogen atoms bonded to one oxygen atom—hence the well-known formula H_2O. The water molecule is bipolar, which means that it has a positive end (pole) and a negative end. Because of these poles, water molecules are able to attract each other rather like magnets. This attraction is called *cohesion*. Cohesion allows water to form drops.

Water can also attract and be attracted to other substances which have bipolar molecules. This attraction is called *adhesion*. Water and soap form bubbles due to this adhesive attraction.

Air takes up room because it is made of molecules. When air is blown into water, it takes up room in the water. The water molecules are attracted to each other and "hold" the air molecules briefly in the form of bubbles on the surface. Adding dishwashing detergent to water changes the attractive force between the water molecules to a stronger adhesive force between the detergent and water molecules. Now, when air is blown in, this adhesive force enables the mixture's molecules to "hold hands" around the air molecules and form longer lasting bubbles. The detergent and water act more like a balloon holding in air.

Cooperative Group Management

Four children can share the group materials, but have the group work in pairs. Each child in the pair takes turns blowing and timing bubbles. The timer should also record timing information so the data sheets do not become totally waterlogged!

Allow the children to work with their partners to complete the conclusion, and then share and compare their conclusion with the other pair at their table.

Call upon a representative from each table to share their results and conclusion for the final discussion. (This is the Partner-Group-Class Sharing cooperative method I referred to in the foreword.)

Materials Needed

1. A handful of sand, sugar, flour, or fine salt.
2. A clear plastic food storage bag.
3. A round balloon.
4. A large clock with second hand (visible to all groups).

For each group
5. A 30 ml medicine measuring cup. (From children's liquid medicines.)

6. A medicine dropper.
7. A small container of dishwashing detergent.

For each child
8. A straw.
9. A 3 ounce paper cup.
10. 30 ml water.
11. Data sheet.

Getting Started

1. Show students a handful of sand, sugar, fine salt, or flour. Point out how easy it is to see what you have in your hand. Ask if it would be as easy to see just one grain.

2. Have the class close their eyes, and tell them that you will be placing one of the grains on a designated table. Ask for a volunteer to then come up and find the grain. (It should be impossible.)

3. Inform the class that all things that take up room are composed of particles even smaller than the grain the volunteer was looking for. Ask them to confer with their partner and come up with a reason why they can't see these particles. Then ask them to share this information with the other pair of children at their table. Ask for a volunteer from each group of four to explain why the particles can't be seen, although they are there. (They are too small.) Tell them that these particles are called *molecules*.

Procedure

1. Illustrate that air is made of molecules by filling a plastic bag with it and having children press on the bag to test that it is full. Blow up a round balloon and ask the children if the air is taking up room in the balloon. What proof can they offer? Then ask if the molecules of the balloon

are "holding hands" around the air. How do they know? Ask if the children think water molecules can hold hands around air molecules in a similar fashion. How would they know? (Bubbles will form on the water.)

2. Ask the children to note their predictions on the data sheet before proceeding to the activity. Each child should note his/her own hypotheses after you allot time for a quick discussion among the groups.

3. Have the children follow the directions on the data sheet.

4. The pairs should share their results with each other before writing their conclusion. Acceptable answers: 1 and 2. hold on to (or attract) each other.

Connections

- **Science:** Lead into a discussion of how tightly molecules bond (hold hands) with each other in a solid as compared to a liquid substance. (You might want to see the lesson The Love Life of Molecules in *Dirt Cheap Science*.)

- **Vocabulary:** Have the class investigate such words as *bond, adhesion, cohesion,* and *Attract*.

- **Technology:** Investigate which detergents have longer lasting bubbles. How do detergents make use of the property of adhesion in cleaning things?

- **Ecology:** What impact upon the environment does the use of detergents have? Are some detergents better for the ecosystem? Why?

- **Reading:** *A Children's Museum Activity Book: Bubbles,* Bernie Zubrowski, illus. Joan Drescher. Little, Boston, 1979 (4–6).

Bubbling Molecules

▲ **PROBLEM:** Do molecules that are alike hold on to each other? Do molecules that are not alike hold on to each other?

■ **HYPOTHESIS:** I think molecules that are alike _____

_____ and unlike molecules will

_____

● **METHOD:**

1. Pour 30 ml of water into paper cup. Place straw in water. Blow gently for 30 seconds.
   —Do bubbles form?
   —Time how long they last.

2. Place 10 drops of detergent into the water. Repeat as above. (*Be sure to blow very gently so you don't splash your eyes.)

🐟 **OBSERVATIONS:**

Mine:
1. Bubbles _____ form.

   They lasted _____

My Partner's:
1. Bubbles _____ form.

   They lasted _____ seconds.

Mine:
2. Bubbles _____ form.

   They lasted _____ seconds.

My Partner's:
2. Bubbles _____ form.

   They lasted _____ seconds.

★ **CONCLUSION:**

1. Molecules that are alike _____

2. Molecules that are not alike _____

Dancing Molecules
Jiggling Jello (followup)

In 40 minutes or less, your physicists will use water and food coloring to discover these . . .

Science Concepts

1. All matter is composed of atoms or molecules which are in constant motion.
2. Warmer molecules have more kinetic (movement) energy than cooler ones, so they move more quickly.
3. Heat energy can cause heated matter to travel to an area with less heat energy. This is called *convection*.

❓ Why Teach This?

Knowing that atoms and molecules are in constant motion (even in solids) and that the warmer a substance is, the more quickly its molecules move, will empower your students to understand why the weather changes. Warm air masses and warm ocean currents move due to the more rapid movement of their molecules.

Students will also find it easier to understand why hot lava flows while relatively cool solid rocks remain where they have been placed!

Cooperative Group Management

This lesson works well with a group of four sharing equipment. Divide the tasks so one child is the official signal giver, two children are the droppers, and the fourth child is the official timer.

Children can work on conclusions using the Partner-Group-Class Sharing method.

Materials Needed

1. Supplies of very cold and very hot water.
2. A large clock with second hand.

For each group

3. Two small clear containers labeled H and C. (Baby food jars are great for this.)
4. Two medicine droppers.
5. A small untippable container of strongly colored food coloring. (No more than 10 ml is necessary.)

For each child

6. Data sheet and followup sheet.

✓ Getting Started

1. Place some papers or plants on a window sill and open the window to allow the wind to make them move. This provides a good inferential clue as you ask the children if air molecules move.
2. Allow the groups time to discuss the question, and then call on each group representative to report their hypothesis.
3. Inform the children that not only do air molecules move, but all molecules move.

   Can they infer which molecules move more quickly—solids or liquids—by looking at their desks and then recalling water in a bathtub? If you think this question is too obvious to spend time on in a group discussion, ask for an individual response followed by a thumb vote.

Announce that today they are going to investigate which molecules move more quickly—hot or cold ones. Allow time for group discussion, but encourage each child to write his/her own hypothesis, using a complete sentence or two.

1 2 3 Procedure

1. To avoid accidents, distribute the food coloring and water after the groups have noted their hypotheses. Be sure each group has an equal amount of hot and cold water in its containers.

   You may wish to briefly discuss why the variables of the quantity of hot and cold water and of food coloring placed in them must be equal. (The only variable being tested is the temperature.)

2. Encourage each child to write a detailed observation after the timers signal that 60 seconds have passed.

   Remind the children to observe both top and side views of each container.

3. The conclusion does not need much group discussion, but allow time for Partner-Group-Class Sharing for the Aha! section. Acceptable conclusion answers: 1. and 2. hot. *Aha!*: 1. move more quickly.

   The Aha! will help the children understand that molecular movement in warm winds and currents makes them flow or move into cooler areas.

   The real life difficulty children experience in making chocolate milk using cold milk and cold syrup will be much more understandable after this lesson.

4. You may wish to use the Jiggling Jello followup (page 20) either as a class activity or as parentally supervised homework.

 **Connections**

- **Social Studies:** Have children research the great ocean currents which travel from the warmer equatorial regions to the cooler polar regions. Ask them to imagine what happens to the movement of the molecules when they reach cooler areas. (They move more slowly and sink, mixing the waters from one region with another.)

  How have warmer currents influenced settlement along the coasts?

- **Life Sciences:** What animals and plants use currents to travel thousands of miles?

- **Geology:** How do ocean currents affect land formations both along the coasts and under the oceans?

  How do lava flows cause changes in the Earth's crust?

- **Technology:** What is the most efficient way to cool a room without air-conditioners or fans? (Open the windows at both top and bottom. This allows warm air, which rises, to escape through the top opening while cool air can flow in through the bottom opening to replace the warm air.)

- **Fire Safety:** Convection of air means that smoke rises. Have the children research and illustrate methods of escaping a fire based upon this fact. Why is it necessary to crawl out of a smoky room?

- **Reading:** *The Invisible World*, Ron Taylor. Facts on File, New York, 1985 (5–7).

Physicist _____

Dancing Molecules

▲ **PROBLEM:** Which molecules move more quickly—hot molecules or cool molecules? Molecules are tiny building blocks, impossible to see with your eyes. Everything is made of them. Even you!

■ **HYPOTHESIS or PREDICTION:** _____

_____

● **METHOD:**

1. Put equal amounts of hot and cold water into two clear containers.
   At the signal, place equally filled droppers of food coloring into each.

2. Observe both containers for 60 seconds. (Look at the side view and the top view.)

✍ **OBSERVATIONS:**

1. _____

   _____

   _____

2. _____

   _____

★ **CONCLUSION:**

1. The food coloring got mixed more quickly in the _____ water.

2. Even though I can't see them, the molecules in the

   _____ water must have had more energy to jump and bump into the food coloring molecules to mix them faster.

AHA!!! _Chocolate syrup is easier to mix in hot milk than cold milk_

because the molecules: _____.

Chef _____

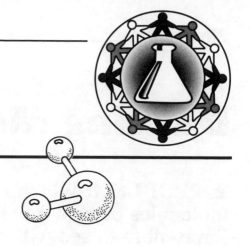

Jiggling Jello!
A Followup to do with Grown-Ups

▲ **PROBLEM:** How can a cook tell when Jello molecules have slowed down?

■ **HYPOTHESIS:** _____

_____

● **METHOD:**

1. Pick your favorite flavor Jello and follow the directions on the box by stirring the powder into the hot water.

2. Refrigerate the Jello. Check it every half-hour to see if the molecules have slowed.

3. Eat the Jello when you can catch the molecules on your spoon.

👁 **OBSERVATIONS:**

1. _____

_____

2. _____

_____

3. _____

_____

★ **CONCLUSION:** I knew the Jello molecules

had slowed down when the jello was _____

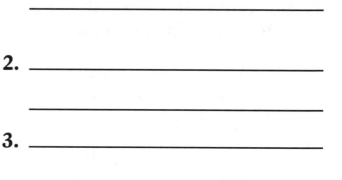

_____

Shake it up, Baby!
(Moving Molecules)

An energetic 45-minute "locomotion" lesson will help your students realize this very important . . .

 Science Concept

1. Energy is never lost, but it can change from one form to another. For example, kinetic energy (energy of movement) can change into heat energy.

? Why Teach This?

The realization that energy can wear many different disguises will empower your students to begin to trace energy as it passes through food chains, sound systems, automobiles, and any other systems which utilize energy.

Cooperative Group Management

This lesson will prove to your scientists how important it is to cooperate with each other in order to complete an experiment.

When you inform the children that they will be shaking a test tube for one minute each, they will tell you that it will be really easy. Once they begin, however, they will soon get tired and long for the next person in the group to take over!

The children will work in groups of four. Student #1 will begin the shaking of test tube A while student #2 holds control test tube B. After one minute they will exchange tubes. After another minute, student #3 will take over the shaking of tube A, and student #4 will take over for the final minute (while stu-

dent #1 continues to hold tube B). At each stage, the two students not holding a tube will keep an eye on the clock and announce the end of the minute.

The success of the activity depends upon the care and skill used in pouring out the two test tubes into the water containers so the temperatures can be recorded.

 **Materials Needed**

1. A large clock with second hand.

For each group
2. A container of room temperature water (about 100 ml).
3. Two thermometers which can be immersed in water. (I prefer thermometers which have both Celsius and Fahrenheit scales so the children can have practice reading each scale.) Label one thermometer A and the other B.
4. Two test tubes with good fitting caps or corks. Label one A and the other B.
5. two small containers (baby jars are great) labeled A and B.

For each child
6. Data sheet.

✓ Getting Started

1. Remind the children that they have just learned that the molecules in hot water move faster than in cold. Do they think that making molecules move would also make them get hotter?
2. Before the children write their hypothesis, you might ask them how they feel after running around in gym for a while. Allow

time for the children to discuss their hypotheses, and then call on a representative to read a hypothesis from each group.

Procedure

1. Have each group place thermometers A and B in the container of water and record the temperatures in the Start box for A and B.

   Make sure that each thermometer is matched with its test tube for the final readings. Often the glass tube on the thermometer has not been placed alongside the scale accurately, so that you may get different readings from two thermometers placed in the same container of water.

   Some of your more observant students may notice such a discrepancy. This can be a good chance to have each group brainstorm why this is so, and you can call upon a representative to explain what the group came up with.

2. After the children have recorded the Start readings, have them place thermometer A in small container A and thermometer B in small container B.

3. Ask if anyone can understand why there has to be a test tube which is just being held. (It is the control in the experiment, and will show what happens to the water without kinetic energy.)

4. Before the children measure the 25 ml of water into each test tube, discuss the fact that they must use a very specific method for holding each test tube. The purpose of this is both to avoid accidents and to avoid heating one tube more than the other with the warmth from a hand. (Explain that this is called controlling the variables, much the same way a race must be fairly run, with everyone starting at the same point.)

   Children should hold the test tubes with their thumb resting securely upon the cork or cap and their fingers grasping the tube as high up as possible.

5. Follow the directions given in the Cooperative Management section for passing the tubes, and urge the children to "Do the Locomotion" or "Shake It Up, Baby." Expect excitement and noise as the children put their all into it.

6. Before the fourth minute of shaking is up, remind the children to be sure to empty tube A into small container A and tube B into small container B.

   After the children have emptied the tubes into the containers, they should read the temperatures and enter them into the Stop box in the observation chart.

   They then calculate and record the differences between the Start and Stop temperatures.

7. Allow the children to work with their partner and share with their group. Then call upon a representative from each group to share each cloze sentence in the conclusion. Acceptable answers are: 1. do or can; 2. heat; 3. change. For *Aha!*: energy.

Connections

• **Technology:** Trace the passage of energy through a car, so the children will realize that plant energy created fossil fuel chemical energy which is being used to create movement energy.

• **Reading:**
Adventures with Atoms and Molecules, Robert C. Mebane and Thomas Rybolt. Enslow, Hillside, NJ, 1985 (4–8).

Also *Adventures with Atoms and Molecules, Part II*, 1987.

Shake it up, Baby!
Molecules do the Locomotion!

▲ **PROBLEM:** If molecules move more when they are hot, would moving them make them get even hotter?

■ **HYPOTHESIS:** _____

● **METHOD:**

1. Record the water temperature in the Start Box for A and B. Use Celsius.

🐛 **OBSERVATION CHART:**

		START	STOP (After 4 minutes)	DIFF. (+ or −)
A	Shake it. (Tested Variable)			
B	Hold it. (Control)			

2. Measure 25 ml of water into tubes A and B. Cap them both.

3. Shake tube **A** hard for four minutes. Hold **B** in one hand and don't shake.

4. Very carefully empty the test tubes into the correct jars and record the *STOP* temperature.

5. Calculate the differences between the START and STOP. Be sure to put a + or − to show if the temperature went up or down.

★ **CONCLUSION:**

1. When molecules move faster, they _____ .

2. Kinetic energy (movement energy) changes into _____ energy.

3. Energy is never lost, but it does _____ form.

AHA! *When our bodies digest food we get chemical* _____ .

Chromatography— An Ink Think!

Magic markers, coffee filters, and water used in a colorful 40-minute lesson will help your chemists deduce the following . . .

Science Concepts

1. The properties of an object depend upon the materials from which it was made.
2. An object made of two or more materials may retain some of their properties, but it may also display new properties.
3. Water has the property of being both cohesive and adhesive.

Why Teach This?

Your chemists will be introduced to chromatography—a method of analyzing a material by separating its components and looking at the colors which emerge during the process.

Cooperative Group Management

This lesson works best with groups of four, but it may be used with smaller groups.

Each child will conduct his/her own analysis of the composition of a specific ink used in a water soluble magic marker. However, the information can be pooled by the group for further detective work when your chemists find the other children who analyzed the same color they did.

Be sure to set a time limit of no more than two minutes for discussion and selection.

Materials Needed

For each group
1. Four water soluble markers of different colors. (Black, brown, green, and blue are good for analysis. Be sure to use the same manufacturer for the same colors. In other words, you can use blues made by Crayola and blacks made by Faber, but don't use blues made by both.)
2. A coffee filter.
3. Two cm rulers.
4. Two scissors.
5. A beaker or jar of water.
6. Four 30 ml measuring cups or baby food jars.
7. Four pencils (*not* pens)

For each child
8. Data sheet.

Getting Started

1. Ask if anyone thinks it is possible for water to overcome gravity, by climbing up a paper towel, for instance.
2. Ask if anyone has ever wondered how different ink colors are made. Allow time for small group discussion and Representative Sharing.

   Does anyone think it might be possible to separate or pull apart ink to see what colors it is made of?

   Invite the children to write a hypothesis based upon the color marker they are going to analyze. (Do not insist that anyone specify a method for pulling ink apart.) If the children seem stumped, you may want to remind them to look at the title of the data sheet for a clue.

4. Each group should select an official group timer.

Procedure

1. Ask the children to read Method 1, look at the equipment on the table, and devise a method for changing the coffee filter into strips (one for each child).

   Providing only two scissors and rulers requires the group to work in a more cooperative manner. They can check each other's measuring skills, as well.

2. Using a pencil, the children should write their initials or name at the very top of the strip.

3. They should measure 5 ml of water into each cup.

   You may wish to discuss the difference between volume—which is measured in either ml or cubic cm—and height—which is measured in linear units such as cm.

4. When children place the dot of color upon the strip, they should center it at a height of 2 cm. (You may wish to place a diagram of this on the board, to avoid confusion.)

5. The chemists now write Observation 1. They should notice that the dot of color spreads out into the surrounding paper even before it is placed in the water.

   Ask if this process is due to cohesion or adhesion. (Adhesion, because it is an attraction between two different substances.)

6. When children place the strip of paper into the water, make sure they do not submerge the dot of color. They should hold the strip so that only its end, below the dot, sits in the water. Otherwise the dot of color will merely dissolve.

7. The official timers are to tell their groups to remove the strips from the water after two minutes.

8. Now, in Observation 2, children should note the colors that separate and state which color travels the farthest up the strip.

9. Before children write the conclusion, refer them once more to the title of the data sheet. Allow time for group discussion and representative sharing about how adhesion and cohesion made the ink and water climb the paper.

   Ask if anyone knows the name of this method of analysis. (Chromatography.)

10. Acceptable conclusion answers are: 1. rose, adhesion; 2. higher or more than the others; 3. chromatography; 4. (depends on colors used), separated or split.

Connections

- **Word Analysis:** What does the prefix *chroma* refer to? What does the suffix *graph* mean?

   Why is a brand name for film "Kodachrome"?

   Challenge the children to discover other words beginning with *chroma-*.

- **Art:** Have your students create coffee filter designs by placing different shades of marker in different sections of the paper, and allowing water to travel up dragging the pigments with them.

- **Consumer Science:** Challenge the groups to analyze markers from different manufacturers. Is the formula for black the same for all?

- **Reading:**
  Experiments with Water, Ray Broekel. Children's Press, Chicago, 1988 (2–4).

Chemist _____

Chromatography:
An Ink Think!

▲ **PROBLEM:** Is it possible to analyze ink in a marker to see how the color was created? How do you think the color of the ink in your marker was made?

■ **HYPOTHESIS:** _____

● **METHOD:**

1. Place a dot • of color 2 cm up from the bottom of a strip of filter paper that measures 6 cm × 2 cm

2. Place the strip with the dotted end into 5 ml of water. *Be sure* the dot is *not* in the water.

👁 **OBSERVATIONS:**

1. The dot _____

   _____

2. The dot _____

   _____

   _____

★ **CONCLUSION:**

1. The water _____ up the paper, pulling the colored

   inks with it because of the attractive force called _____.

2. Some colors were attracted to the water more strongly, so they

   climbed _____.

3. Analyzing a substance by looking at the colors of the materials

   it is made from is called _____.

4. My color ink, _____, was made of _____.

   I know this because chromatography _____ the ink into its component colors.

Plant Pipes—Tying it all Together!
The Great Xylem Race (followup)

Your physicists will make the leap into botany in a 40-minute lesson which dramatically illustrates how water can travel against gravity! It also illustrates these . . .

Science Concepts

1. Water molecules attract each other with a force called *cohesion.*
2. Water molecules are attracted to other types of molecules with a force called *adhesion.*
3. Living things have properties (adaptations) which help them survive.
4. A system occurs when two or more objects work together. Energy and matter interact within a system.

Why Teach This?

This lesson allows you to help the children transfer knowledge from one discipline of science to another, reinforcing the concept that "everything is connected to everything."

Understanding that events on a molecular level influence events on a larger scale is a powerful idea. It will lead your students to look for underlying causes in other situations as well.

Cooperative Group Management

This lesson is easily handled by groups of two, three, or four children, depending upon how much equipment you possess. I usually provide equipment for a group of four.

Allow time for the groups to discuss the reasoning for their hypotheses before writing thcm. Call on a representative from each group to share, and use thumb votes to see who agrees or disagrees with the hypothesis being shared.

While the experiment is taking place, there will be time for children to discuss further if they agree or disagree with the offered hypotheses.

The tasks of the experiment can be divided as follows: One child measures out the 30 ml of water, one child tells the pourer when to stop, the third child places the strip in position, and the fourth child is the official timer.

Materials Needed

For each group
1. Two 30 ml measuring cups or baby food jars.
2. A pourable container of water.
3. A strip of felt approximately 1 cm wide and 6–8 cm long.

For each child
4. Data sheet.

Getting Started

1. Before the children hypothesize, remind them of what they learned earlier (page 14): how bubbles form when water molecules and detergent molecules attract each other, and how molecules of water can attract each other as well.

Direct children's attention to the data sheet diagram of cups A and B, with the felt strip going from one to the other. Ask them if they think the water could travel from container A to B without being poured.

Allow discussion time before the hypotheses are committed to paper.

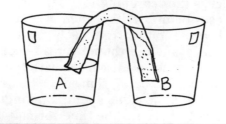

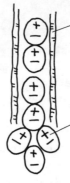

Procedure

1. Follow Method step 1. The children can take turns feeling the felt strip, and will notice that the water climbs to make the strip wet.

   During this three- to five-minute time period, try to elicit that the water is overcoming the force of gravity because it is traveling upward on the strip.

2. Depending upon the thickness of the felt, water will begin to appear in Cup B within about five minutes.

   If some Cup Bs are filling faster than others, ask why this is happening. Allow group discussion and representative sharing. (You probably have not controlled the variables of the width and length of the felt strip. In fact, I vary the size of the strips on purpose, to give the children a chance to see how important it is to control each variable except the one being tested.)

3. The conclusion should be written after you again remind the children that water attracts water and other substances, too.

   Sketch some water molecule models on the board, with pluses and minuses to illustrate their poles and to show how they can attract each other. (You may wish to mention that this is the force called cohesion.) Sketch water molecules traveling through a thin tube or pipe to show how they are attracted to that, as well. (This, of course, is the force called adhesion.)

The water molecules are attracted to the walls or fibers of the fabric or plant stems (adhesion).

Water molecule—the plus and minus poles attract each other (cohesion).

Allow group discussion and writing, followed by Representative Sharing.

The conclusion can be completed as follows: 1. can; 2. gravity; 3. molecules; 4. felt

4. The *Aha!* Section foreshadows The Great Xylem Race followup (page 30). Most children know that water must travel to the topmost leaves of a plant, and overcome gravity to do so. The cloze answer: tubes or pipes.

Connections

- **Consumerism:** Encourage your consumer scientists to develop a test for which paper towel is the "better picker-upper."

- **Ecology:** How can muddy water be cleaned using the same method as in the experiment? Can matter travel through the felt with the water, or can it be separated? How can this knowledge help campers?

Plant Pipes—
Tying it all Together

▲ **PROBLEM:** How can water overcome gravity to climb plant stems?

■ **HYPOTHESIS:** _____

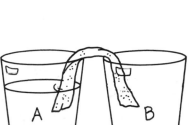

_____

● **METHOD:**

1. Fill bowl **A** with 30 ml of water. Place the fabric strip so it hangs into both bowls. Watch the strip and feel it. What does the water do?

2. Wait 5 minutes. What happens during this time period?

🐚 **OBSERVATIONS:**

1. _____

_____

_____

2. _____

_____

★ **CONCLUSION:**

1. Water _____ be moved without pouring it.

2. Water can even overcome the force of _____.

3. Molecules of water can attract other water _____, and this force is called *cohesion.*

4. Molecules of water were also attracted to the thin tubes or

pipes in the _____. This force is called *adhesion.*

AHA! *If water can travel up a plant stem, there probably are*

_____ *in the stem, so the water won't slide back down!*

The Great "Xylem" Race! (followup)

MATERIALS:

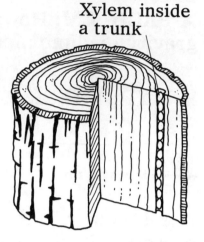

Xylem inside a trunk

- You will need a 6–8 cm strip of celery and a broccoli stem. Make sure they are the *same length*. Their width can be about 2 cm. They are the race contestants!

- A small container of water colored deeply by food coloring.

READY, SET, GO! Place the 2 stems into the (colored) water.

■ **PREDICT:** What do you think the water will do to the stems? __

_____

WAIT: Keep checking until you see a change. What happened?

☞ OBSERVATIONS: _____

_____

★ **CONCLUSION:**

1. The water _____ the _____
   part of the stems.   inner or outer

2. There are _____ in the stems, just like the pipes in the fabric strip. These pipes are narrow to help water

   overcome _____ .

4. These plant pipes are called _____ .

5. Which plant was the winner of the *Xylem Race?* _____ .

Leaf It To Chromatography
Green Plants—What We Know and What We've Learned (pre-lesson and followup chart)

Recommended for Grades 3 and above

Your chemists will use chromatography to discover the chemicals present in a leaf, including those not normally visible. This 50-minute lesson will lead to mastery of the following . . .

Science Concepts

1. Green plants are adapted for survival because they possess the chemical called *chlorophyll*, which enables them to capture sunlight and utilize it for food production.
2. Green plants are found at the beginning of food chains because only they can produce food through the process of photosynthesis.

Why Teach This?

By the time students reach third grade, they may have been taught that green plants produce their own food. However, I have found that this concept is extremely difficult for children (and some adults) to believe.

Giving children the opportunity to see the chemicals found in leaves will allow you to review the process of photosynthesis in a unique way. Your children will actually see the chlorophyll climb the filter paper, along with the other chemicals which give deciduous leaves their beautiful fall colors.

If your community is in an area where leaves change color, I recommend doing this lesson in the fall.

This will enable you to show the children leaves which are no longer able to capture sunlight in order to perform photosynthesis to produce their own food (sugar).

Holding up a brown or yellow leaf which has lost its chlorophyll will enable you to discuss why deciduous leaves must fall off trees in autumn. The loss of chlorophyll makes the leaf die, causing it to fall, and this prevents the tree from losing much water during the winter.

This lesson will also help the children realize that a plant is a system, because its parts work together. The roots absorb water through adhesion and cohesion, and the xylem transports this water up to the leaves, where it is combined with carbon dioxide to form simple sugar. The chlorophyll in the leaf captures the sunlight to provide the energy for the rearrangement of water and carbon dioxide molecules into the larger sugar molecule.

Cooperative Group Management

This lesson points up the advantage of cooperation because it requires a lot of physical work. I recommend groups of four not only because a lot of leaf grinding is necessary, but also to cut down on the amount of acetone or alcohol used.

Try to begin with the chart Green Plants—What We Know and What We Learned (page 35), giving time for the groups to partner, group, and class share information they already have.

If you find that your class is really deficient in knowledge, you may wish to have them complete the lesson Eat Your Way Through Botany in *Dirt Cheap Science*.

Materials Needed

1. A dropper.
2. A bottle of acetone (nail polish remover) or rubbing alcohol. (I prefer the acetone because it climbs the paper and separates the chemicals more quickly.) **NOTE: You should do the dispensing of the acetone or alcohol, and there should be good ventilation in the room. Be sure to cap the substance to avoid excess evaporation. These common household substances are flammable and should be handled with care.**
3. A baby food jar or 30 ml measuring cup.
4. (optional) Red, yellow, orange, and green chalk.

For each group
5. A spinach or beet leaf. (You can use leaves from outdoors, but be sure they are not leathery in texture and therefore too difficult to grind.)
6. Mortar and pestle. (You may be able to borrow some from your high school. If not, find some small, heavy crockery bowls, and have the children use the end of a plastic test tube or Lincoln Log to grind the leaves.)
7. A flat ended toothpick or splint.
8. A 6 × 1 cm strip of filter or chromatography paper.

For each child
9. Data sheet and review sheet.

Getting Started

1. If you begin with the review chart, allot about ten minutes for discussion and writing. You can stimulate the discussion by asking pointed questions about specific plant parts such as roots, stems, leaves, flowers, and seeds and what their functions are. Be sure to ask questions which relate plants to the environment and lead to the review of oxygen production, prevention of soil erosion, and food chains.
2. Remind the children of their prior experience with chromatography (page 24) and ask if there might be a way to analyze the chemicals in a leaf. Give time for Group Sharing before the hypothesis is written.

Procedure

1. The group needs to grind no more than a small portion (about 3 × 3 cm) of a leaf for good results.

    Each group member can tear a section of the leaf into the tiniest possible pieces and then take turns grinding all of the pieces together.
2. While the children are grinding, place 5–10 drops of solvent into the mortar or bowl. This will facilitate the release of the chemicals from the leaf. At this time, the children should initial the end of their strip of filter paper.
3. When the mashed leaves are a soupy green, have the students use a toothpick or splint to place and press the mixture onto the

filter strip about 2 cm up from the bottom. The more intense the color they press onto the paper, the more impressive the results will be.

4. Pour solvent into your measuring cup or jar to a height of about 1 cm. Each group's representative should then place their initialed strip into the jar.

5. The solvent will climb up the strips because of adhesion and cohesion, and the chemicals in the leaves will begin to be dragged along, the way the inks were (see page 26). The chemicals will begin to separate as some are dragged more easily than others.

   A new representative should bring the group's strip back after 5 minutes.

   A green color indicates chlorophyll, yellow indicates xanthophyll, red is anthocyanin, and orange is carotene.

   If you have the colored chalks, you might wish to write the names of the chemicals in the corresponding colors on the board.

6. Conclusion answers: 1. chromatography; 2. chlorophyll, food or sugar, light; 3. anthocyanin, yellow, carotene.

   Allow time for group discussion and representative sharing of the conclusion.

7. Have students complete the What We Learned section of the review sheet. Then have students work in their groups on the word maps at the bottom of the sheet.

Connections

- **Art:** The children collect leaves before they turn color. Then they place a leaf on a sheet of white paper and write or draw on the leaf. The pressure of the pencil will force the different chemicals onto the white paper, so the children can see what chemicals are in the leaf, as well as create a design.

- **Ecology:** To find out what dead leaves are good for, go on a walk to look for piles of leaves which gather along fences or in corners of the school yard. The children will see the leaves decomposing and becoming an enriching part of the soil. Research into carnivores' food chains will always lead the children back to green plants.

- **Reading:**
  Tree, David Burnie. Knopf, New York, 1988 (4–8).

  I Found a Leaf, Sharon Lerner. Lerner, Minneapolis, 1967 (2–4).

  How Leaves Change, Sylvia A. Johnson. Lerner, Minneapolis, 1986 (3–5).

Leaf Chromatography!

▲ **PROBLEM:** How can we analyze a leaf to see what chemicals are in it?

■ **HYPOTHESIS:** _____

● **METHOD:**

1. Grind a small quantity of leaf bits. Mix with solvent and grind till "soupy."

2. All pencil your initials at the top of the paper strip. Then place a dot • of soupy mush on the strip 2 cm from the bottom.
   Place the strip in your teacher's jar of solvent. Wait.

👁 **OBSERVATIONS:**

1. _____

   _____

2. _____

   _____

   _____

★ **CONCLUSION:**

1. _____ was the method we used to separate the chemicals in a leaf.

2. _____ was the green chemical found the most because it helps green plants make _____ during photosynthesis by absorbing _____.

3. Leaves that turn red in the fall have _____ while leaves that have lots of xanthophyll will turn _____. Orange leaves have _____ just like carrots!

Green Plants Summary

What We Know	What We Learned!
_____	_____
_____	_____
_____	_____
_____	_____
_____	_____
_____	_____
_____	_____
_____	_____
_____	_____

Try to take all your information and make a word map about plants on a separate sheet with your group. Here's an idea of how to do it . . .

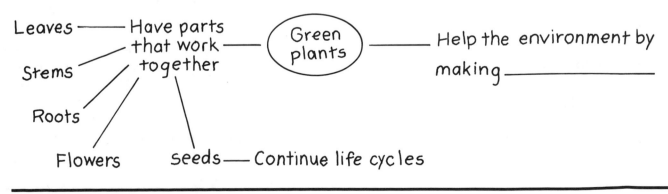

Tree Rings: Clues to the Past!

Tree Cookie Stumpers (followup)

In a 30-minute lesson, your students will become dendrologists in order to discover what the environment was like in the past. They will also discover these . . .

Science Concepts

1. Environmental conditions in an area affect the condition of the organisms that live there.
2. Living things have adaptations or properties which help them survive.
3. Organisms must also adapt to changes in their environment in order to survive those changes.

? Why Teach This?

Children must understand that "everything is connected to everything" in order to become citizens capable of protecting the environment.

The study of tree rings gives a graphic idea of how living things are affected by environmental factors such as rainfall, sunlight, and access to clean air. A tree growing today in an urban environment of smog and limited sunlight will not achieve the growth of a tree in an unpolluted area.

By substituting humans for trees one can see why it is important for children to understand the need for protecting the environment.

Cooperative Group Management

This lesson is easily handled by groups of four, in terms of equipment.

During discussion and calculation times, have the children work with partners and then check their calculations with their group.

Calculations will be different for each group, because they will each have a different tree cookie or core to deal with. However, group representatives can share the general conclusion with the entire class.

Materials Needed

For each group
1. A tree cookie (a 2-3 inch cross-section cut from a trunk of a tree). You can obtain tree cookies from firewood dealers—ask for a selection from different logs, if possible. If you cannot obtain tree cookies, you can use:

- tree stumps on your school property;

- teacher-made tree core specimens. Real tree cores are samples of the tree's radius cut out by a cylindrical drill. You can make imitation cores by using a thin-line permanent marker to draw rings around as many full size pencils as you need for your groups.

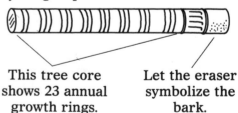

This tree core shows 23 annual growth rings.   Let the eraser symbolize the bark.

For each child
2. Data sheet.

1. Refresh the children's memory of the purpose of xylem in a plant or tree trunk.

2. Inform the children that besides having pipes of xylem, trees annually grow a new layer of wood just under the bark. This layer, called *cambium*, has tubes which carry food down to the roots for storage for rainy days and early spring time. Cambium becomes xylem when another layer grows over it during the next year of the tree's life. This process makes rings which can be seen in a tree stump.

3. Quickly review the purpose of bark—to protect the tree from insects and weather. Ask for an analogy in human bodies. (Bark is to a tree as *skin* is to a human body.)

4. Ask what would happen to children who didn't get the proper nourishment. What do they think would happen to the growth of a new cambium ring in a tree if it didn't get the proper amount of sunlight or water it needed that year to perform photosynthesis and make its food?

   Allow time for group discussion, and then direct the dendrologists (scientists who study tree rings) to write their hypotheses.

Procedure

1. Give each group a tree cookie to examine. Are the rings all the same width? Is there a pattern of several narrow rings and then a few wide rings?

   Have the children write their observations of the rings and any pattern they discern.

2. A dark ring appears for summer, and a light ring appears for spring, so the children should count only the light rings to see how many rings there are.

   Ask if anyone knows how to calculate when their tree started its first year of growth. (The present year minus the number of rings.)

3. Conclusion: when there were narrow light rings, the tree's environment did not offer what it needed due to crowding in a forest, or the lack of rain in drought years, for example.

   Each group should be able to calculate how old its tree was if you tell them it was cut down this year, and should also be able to state whether it grew in an environment which was generally good or poor for it.

4. When rings are wider on one side than the other, it may mean that the tree was on a hill and grew more wood on that side.

Connections

- **Social Studies:** Have the children make a timeline starting from the year their tree began its growth, noting local and national events and checking to see what kind of growth their tree had in those years.

- **Ecology:** How do trees affect the environment? Review the previous lesson (page 35), and have the children brainstorm all the ways trees positively interact with their community.

- **Reading:**
  Discovering Trees, Douglas Florian. Macmillan, New York, 1986 (1–3).

  Oak and Company, Richard Mabey. Greenwillow, New York, 1983 (2–5).

Dendrologist _____

Tree Rings: Clues to the Past!

▲ **PROBLEM:** Can a tree's rings tell us about the environmental conditions it grew in? How?

■ **HYPOTHESIS:** _____

● **METHOD:**

1. Examine the tree cookie . . . or core to see if all the lighter rings are the same width.

2. Can you find a pattern . . . of thick rings and narrow rings?

3. Count the lighter rings . . . How many are there? Calculate to find what year your tree began its growth.

👁 **OBSERVATIONS:**

1. _____

_____

2. _____

_____

3. _____

_____

★ **CONCLUSION:**

1. Our tree's rings _____ all the same width, so the amount of available water and sunlight was _____ in different years.

2. Our tree was _____ years old, and began growth in the year _____. For the first decade of the tree's life environmental conditions were probably _____.

THINK . . .

What conditions besides sunlight and water could affect a tree's growth pattern?

Tree Cookie Stumpers!

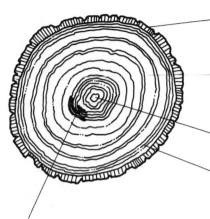

Bark—protects the tree from insects, disease and weather

Sapwood (Xylem)—carries water and sap up from roots

Heartwood—Older wood that gives a tree strength

Cambium layer—carries food to all parts of tree

Scar shows fire damage.

This tree was 16 years old when it was cut down.
It had 5 years of good rainfall and sunlight.

Now . . . Draw your own tree cookie. Label it with the proper tree trunk vocabulary. Write its age and a few sentences about its history on the back of this sheet. Show it to your partner and see if they can tell you about it . . . or are they stumped?

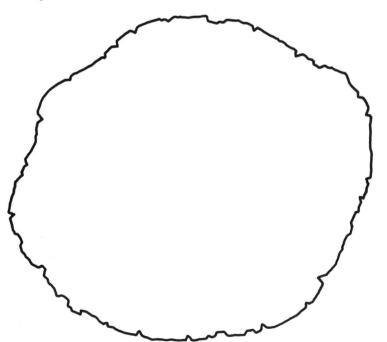

Weed Wonders
Mini Weed and Seed Guide Booklet
(reference)

A 50-minute walk around your school grounds will provide your botanists with an easily accessible, no-cost source of plants so they can discover these . . .

Science Concepts

1. Plants are systems composed of specialized parts which work together.
2. An ecosystem occurs when living and nonliving things interact and affect one another.
3. Organisms which are well adapted to their environment survive and are able to complete their life cycle so the species survives.
4. The introduction of a species into an environment where it does not have a natural enemy may cause negative changes in the existing community.

Why Teach This?

The definition of a *weed* is a plant in a place where it is not wanted. Many weeds in the United States were introduced from Europe in hopes that they would be valuable food sources for humans and cattle. Kudzu, an Asian plant, was introduced into the southern United States as a ground cover, and because it has no natural enemy or source of control, it has become an extremely invasive plant which grows over anything that stands still long enough!

Plants which are not wanted can be harmful to agriculture in several ways. They compete with wanted plants for water and minerals. They cost farmers and gardeners money for eradication. They cause the use of herbicides which may be detrimental to groundwater and animal life. Aquatic weeds may choke waterways and impede navigation of boats and animals.

At the same time, weeds can be valuable when they produce seeds for birds, or prevent erosion with their tenacious root systems in areas where other plants cannot survive.

They are valuable for study also because they provide wonderful examples of adaptations (properties which help organisms survive). Some of the most common weeds, such as broadleaf plantain and little hop-clover (famous as the Irish shamrock), grow so low that they escape the lawnmower's blades.

Weeds are usually extremely prolific in seed production, another reason they are so successful. They can travel as windblown parachutes or as hitch-hikers with hooks or burrs. Seeds may also remain dormant for years, until growing conditions are good. The study of weeds and their seed dispersal can be generalized to other plants, so your students can recognize how they continue their life cycles with seed dispersal.

Additionally, the study of weeds can lead to the understanding of succession. Many weeds are pioneer plants in areas where nothing else can live. Animals can feast upon their seeds and further enliven the area. When the animals and weeds die, they decompose to enrich the soil, paving the way for other species of plants.

Cooperative Group Management

For your initial in-class discussion, have the children work in groups of two, three, or four.

For your outdoor work, have the children work in pairs.

 ## Materials Needed

1. Access to any outdoor area on or near your school grounds. (A small untended area is best.)

For each group

2. As many trowels as you can borrow. (Metal soup spoons can substitute.)

3. (optional) A plastic sandwich bag for the weed.

For each student

4. Data sheet and weed guide. (Pages 44–46. Have students cut on the dotted lines and staple pages together by one corner.)

 ## Getting Started

1. Have the children review their plant word maps or chart and then ask if anyone knows what a weed is. Explain that they are going on a hunt for weeds, and so they have to know where to look and what to look for.

   Allow time for group discussion before the hypothesis is written. Explain that the children will be using trowels (or spoons) to dig up weeds to be studied in the classroom.

2. Elicit that weeds grow in places other plants frequently do not— such as cracks in sidewalks and alongside the foundations of buildings. They can be recognized as looking different from most plants that have been purposely grown, such as lawn grass.

3. Emphasize that the children must remove nothing from the ground unless you approve. **Review what poison ivy looks like before you go out!**

4. Assign partners, or have the children select their own if you feel they can do so effectively.

Procedure

1. Take the class on a general tour of the school grounds, so they can note all the places where they find weeds. The locations and brief descriptions can be noted in Observation 1.

2. When you get to an area where there are sufficient weeds for each pair to be able to dig out one, have the gardeners tug gently on the stems to see how the roots hold firmly into the ground.

   Observation 2 should reflect that the roots are difficult to remove and have multi-shoots. Inform the children that many weeds will regrow if part of the root is left in the ground. (Dandelions are a terrific weed for illustrating this point.)

   Have the children notice how soil clings to the roots, so they can infer that plants' roots can prevent erosion by wind and water.

3. You may elect to do Observation 3 back in class. "Baggies" are good for saving the weeds if you have to finish the activity later during the day.

   This observation asks for a sketch of the weed and a labeling of its parts. If any weeds have flowers, ask what the job of the flower is. (To produce seeds.)

   If anyone finds weeds with seed pods or seedheads, be sure that everyone has a chance to figure out what "travel agent" the seeds use to get around!

Have the children refer to their Mini-Weed Guides for help in identifying seed types and possible common species.

4. Conclusion 1 requires the children to infer why the weed was able to live where it was found. Have them brainstorm clues. (Root strength, general size, height of stem, number of seeds produced, and texture of leaves—if leathery or tough, the weed could live with less water.)

Allow time for sharing of observations so the children can pool their information. They should be able to realize that weeds are able to grow where they can because they are well adapted and don't have many natural enemies.

Other conclusion answers:
2. seeds, travel, plants.

5. The *Aha!* Section asks the children to realize that while weeds may not be where we want them to be, they can be a vital part of the ecosystem as food for birds and small mammals, as well as binders of soil. Answers: edible or eaten, erosion.

◤ Connections

- **Science:** Can an animal be a weed? Ask children to transfer what they have learned about weeds to the problem of animals from one ecosystem being introduced into another without its natural enemies.

They can research what happened when gypsy moths were introduced as the great hope of the American silk industry. The migration of African bees (known as killer bees) and the brown tree snake of Guam are other subjects of interest.

- **More Science:** Have the children collect as many weeds as possible, identify them with a weed field guide (from your school or public library), and add their sketches to their Mini-Weed Guides.

- **Reading:**
Weeds—A Golden Guide; Alexander C. Martin. Golden Press, New York, 1972 (2 up).

Weeds and Wildflowers, Illa Podendorf. Children's Press, Chicago, 1981 (2–3).

Weeds—A Golden Guide, Alexander C. Martin. Golden Press, New York, 1972 (all ages).

Weed Wonders!

▲ **PROBLEM:** What are weeds, and where can they be found?

■ **HYPOTHESIS:** _____

_____

● **METHOD:** ☜ **OBSERVATIONS:**

1. As you walk, list all the places you notice weeds on the back of this page.

2. a. Was it very easy or difficult to remove your weed? How did you do it?
   b. Did the root have one piece or several sections?

2. a. _____

_____

b. _____

_____

3. Sketch your weed on the back of this page. Label its parts.

★ **CONCLUSION:**

1. My weed is a plant that can live in _____

because _____

2. Weeds can be found in so many places because they make so

many _____, and these can _____ in

so many different ways. They can crowd out wanted _____.

AHA! *Weeds can be helpful to birds because their seeds are* _____,

and weeds help the Earth's soil by preventing _____.

Weed Wonders

My Mini Weed and Seed Field Guide!

Naturalist _____

Weeds use different types of "travel agents" to spread their seeds so they can continue their life cycles.

Some seeds hitch-hike on animals' fur.

Pitchfork   Cocklebur

Others ride the wind with "parachutes."

Others are so tiny, they don't need any help to ride the wind.

2

Poison Ivy is a weed that can trick you because it grows as a vine or as a small shrub.

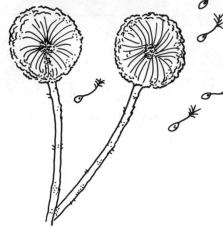

Its leaves can be shiny—but not always! Don't touch them.

If you touch any part of the weed you can develop a rash.

If you are not sure it is poison ivy, DON'T TOUCH!

3

Little Hop-Clover is the plant you might call a shamrock.

It grows so low it escapes the blades of the lawnmower. Its seeds are extremely small

This weed is found mostly in lawns, gardens, and pastures.

4

Weed Wonders

Small Crabgrass sprouts from seeds to live in your lawn and spoil its appearance.

When it dies in winter, it leaves brown patches that look even worse!

5

Wild Onion is also called onion grass.

You can tell it's there because when the grass is cut you will smell onions!

When onion grass gets into grain fields, the seeds get mixed into the grain. This can spoil the flour because it will smell like onions!

6

Spurge is a plant that loves to hug the ground.

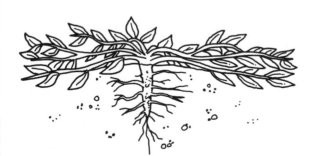

It makes so many tiny seeds that it is very difficult to get rid of.

7

Queen Anne's Lace is related to the carrots you eat.

It has flowers which look very lacy, and have a tiny purple blossom in the center of the flower head.

Its seeds have little hooks to hitch rides on animals so they can spread to good growing areas.

This weed grows in fields and along roads.

8

Weed Wonders

Milkweed is a weed which spreads with many "parachute" seeds that float through the air.

Butterflies love milkweed, but if you want to get rid of it, you'd better do it before the seed pods open and the seeds begin their flight.

9

Mullein has very fuzzy dull green leaves that lie close to the ground.

After a year, it sends up a long stem which has small yellow flowers at the very top of it.

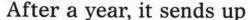

These weeds grow on land where other plants can't, so they can help prevent erosion.

10

Plantains are a big problem in lawns.

Their flower spike produces pollen which causes people to sneeze with hay fever.

They are very difficult to dig up.

11

Chicory is known as a wildflower when it flowers with its attractive blue blossoms.

It grows along roads, vacant lots and fields.

Chicory is sometimes added to coffee.

When it grows where it is not wanted, that's when it is called a weed!

12

All About Changes: A Succession Hunt!
Successions: A Home Hunt (followup)

Your ecologists will develop their observation and inference skills as they learn to recognize environmental changes. This will occur during a 10-minute pre-walk discussion, a 30-minute walk through your school grounds, and a 10-minute post-walk discussion. Along the way they will also discover these . . .

Science Concepts

1. Living things affect and are affected by their environment.
2. When living things and the physical environment interact, they form what is called an *ecosystem*.
3. A *community* is a group of plants and animals which depend upon each other in the area they share.
4. A change in the ecosystem which causes another change is called a *succession*.

Why Teach This?

When your students understand that one change may cause many changes in the environment, including some we may not have the power to foresee, they may become more sensitive to the need to preserve the Earth ecosystem of which they form part.

When Earth Day is celebrated in April, your students will truly understand the meaning behind it.

Cooperative Group Management

For the classroom discussion, groups of four will be fine for Partner, Group, and Representative Sharing.

The outside walk is best handled by partners working together. It would be helpful to select partners who do not sit together during the discussions, because then there will be a greater exchange of information about different parts of the school environment.

Materials Needed

1. Various outdoor areas around your school—blacktop, lawn, treed areas, along fences, etc.

For each student
2. Data sheet.

Getting Started

1. I like to start off with this message on the board: "Welcome to a great day in science. You will see a series of successes today!" Be sure to define *series* as one thing following another.
2. Give time for a quick discussion of what *community* means. Ask the group to suggest who lives in their community, and who they depend on. Do the community members depend upon them? (If a child states, for example, that the children depend upon firemen to keep them safe, remind them that firemen depend upon the people in the community for their jobs.) Be sure to establish the fact that members of a community depend upon each other.
3. Can anyone think of something in the community which has

changed recently? Have new homes been built? Will this generate the need for more community services? Will the change in the community create a series of changes? Allow time for group discussion and representative sharing.

4. Ask the children to imagine a forest as a community. What would be the living members of that community? Allow time for each group to make a quick word map of a forest community. Be sure that they do not overlook trees and plants.

   What do they think the physical factors would be like in the forest? Would it be shady? Would the soil be sandy or dark and loamy? Do they think that these factors would influence the type of living members found in that community?

5. What would happen if there was a forest fire? Do the children think there would be a change? Would that change cause a series of changes?

   Explain that when one change causes another in nature, we call that *succession*.

   Expect your students to list all the negatives associated with forest fires. Point out, however, that naturally caused forest fires help seeds which need heat to germinate.

6. Explain that the class is going to take a tour around the school to see if they can find any clues to past and ongoing changes in natural succession.

1 2 3 Procedure

1. As you tour the grounds, many children may recall that weeds grow in cracks in pavement. Find these areas, and be sure to notice if the weeds are breaking up the concrete. Ask what will happen if the weeds are not removed. Will the cracks stay the same?

   Be sure to have your ecologists list the members of the "pavement community" and discuss the physical factors of sunlight and water availability. Explain that this "pavement community" is really an ecosystem because the plants and any other organisms are interacting with the physical factors of the environment.

   If you see insects, try to elicit that even though the insect may not be eating the plants, there must be a food chain present.

   Don't forget to look at nearby buildings and try to decide if the area will be shady during part of the day. Have the children list the physical factors in the proper place on the data sheet.

   After this brief discussion, allow the partners to fan out into the area to look for evidence of successions going on.

   If you are pressed for time, you may have the children complete the Successions column for homework.

2. If you have any wooded areas, be sure to check under fallen logs for community members such as sowbugs, worms, snails, slugs, and fungi which will help the log to decay. Ask the children how rain will further change the log. (It will soften it, helping it to decay.)

   What will happen to the community of animals and fungi when the log finally decomposes? How will the log affect the soil? (It will enrich it, enabling another plant to succeed.)

   What food chains or webs are suggested by the evidence?

   Once again, try to allow the partners to investigate nearby

areas. Remind them to note the physical factors of the area.

3. Another good area to check is along fences and in corners where the wind or gardeners blow leaves. Look under piles to see communities similar to those listed in #2.

4. If you have any small ponds nearby, take a trip there. Are there trees? Do their leaves fall into the pond? Note the physical factors of the area. What will happen when the leaves decompose? (The soil will gradually build up until the pond is no longer depressed and rain will no longer drain into it.) What will grow now in the soil which used to be a pond? (Pioneer weeds.) What will succeed next? (Seeds blown from nearby trees.) Will the community members have changed the physical factors?

5. Back in the classroom, allow the children to compare their discoveries with one another.

Allow time for discussion of further successions which might occur. Be sure to require good evidence to back up these statements.

The class should reach the conclusion that ecosystems are constantly changing, whether due to natural or human-made causes.

 Connections

- **Science:** Successions: A Home Hunt followup (page 51) can be assigned as homework. If necessary, review what the children learned to look for in the school hunt. The cloze answers in the review sentence: Succession, changes.

- **Science and Art:** Why are ecologists worried about global warming? What successions are they predicting? How are Vermont's sugar maple trees endangered by factories in the Midwest? What successions are taking place in our waterways as a result of pollution? What changes can we expect next?

Research on these questions will prepare your students so they can create informative posters.

- **Social Studies:** What is the history of your school? What was there before your school was built? How have changes in your community caused changes in your school?

Make a timeline which shows how one change in the community led to a succession of changes that make your school and community what it is today.

- **Reading:**

A Forest is Reborn, James R. Newton, 1982. Harper, New York (2–4).

Chains, Webs and Pyramids, The Flow of Energy In Nature, Laurence Pringle. 1975 Harper, New York (4–7).

Moon-Dark, Patricia Wrightson. Macmillan, New York, 1988 (5–8). A fictional account of human-caused ecological imbalances.

All About Changes: A Succession Hunt!

An _____ is a system which connects living members of a community with the physical environment of sunlight, water, air, and soil.

What ecosystems can you find around school? Have they always been the same? Will they change?

PHYSICAL FACTORS and LOCATION	COMMUNITY MEMBERS	SUCCESSION? WHY?
Where is the ecosystem? What are its physical factors?	Name the plants and animals living together and depending on each other.	What was the area like a while ago? What will it be like as time goes by?
		_____ _____
		_____ _____
		_____ _____

Successions: A Home Hunt! (Followup)

_____ happen when a change in an ecosystem causes

other _____ to occur.

1. What ecosystems can you find around your home? Name them in the LOCATION section. Describe the sunlight, soil, and amount of moisture.
2. What living things did you find? List them in the COMMUNITY section.
3. Do you think the ecosystem was always as it is now? Will it change more? Explain your thinking in the SUCCESSION section.

PHYSICAL FACTORS and LOCATION	COMMUNITY MEMBERS	SUCCESSION? WHY?
		_____ _____
		_____ _____
		_____ _____
		_____ _____

Flying Fungus and Marching Mushrooms
Friendly Fungus Physical Factors (Followup)

A two-part 40-minute lesson recreating conditions in a forest will help your ecologists realize these . . .

Science Concepts

1. Organisms have special properties or adaptations for survival, and will grow or flourish when environmental conditions are correct for those adaptations.
2. All organisms must have a means of completing a life cycle. The production of spores by fungi enables the continuation of their life cycle.
3. Green plants provide the basic food supply in an area because only they possess the chlorophyll necessary for photosynthesis. Plants which do not possess chlorophyll must get food from another source.
4. Decomposers are a vital part of ecosystems, because they break down dead organisms into basic nutrients and energy that can be used or recycled by living organisms.

Why Teach This?

Letting children learn that nature recycles the matter from which everything is made is a great way to help them understand that we must also recycle human-made materials.

Normally, diagrams of a food chain do not include decomposers at the end. Yet when carnivores die without being eaten by another carnivore, they decompose. I feel that children should understand that the final consumer in the food chain is a decomposer, which contributes to the ecosystem by returning nutrients to the soil.

Cooperative Group Management

Groups of four make this an easily managed lesson. It will enable you to have each group find a different place to test for the presence of spores, and at least one child in each group should be able to bring in one or more edible mushrooms for spore printing.

The children may partner-group-class share for the pre-experiment discussion. **Caution: Do not allow children to eat wild mushrooms!**

Materials Needed

1. Heavy white paper (for spore prints).
2. A small branch with fungus growing on it.
3. A handful of samaras (any seeds with attached wings such as maple keys).

For each group
4. One or more **edible** mushrooms.
5. A hand lens.
6. A small piece of bread (4 × 4 cm).
7. A container of water.
8. A dropper.
9. A plastic sandwich bag or disposable petri dish.
10. A label.
11. Tape for sealing the bag and attaching the label to it.

For each child
12. Data sheet.

1. Two days before you plan to teach this lesson, have volunteers bring in mushrooms.

   Model how to gently remove the covering over the gills of the mushroom so they become visible. Allow time for sketching the underside of the cap.

   Model: Remove the stem from each group's mushroom, and place the mushroom gill-side down onto a piece of heavy white paper in an area that will not be disturbed. Do not volunteer any information about why you are doing this.

2. After a day or two, check to see if any dark smudges conforming to the gill pattern and shape of the mushroom appear on the paper. If so, you have made a spore print and are now ready to proceed with the discussion.

3. Remind the children of their walks to find weeds and eco-systems (Weed Wonders, page 43.) Ask what happens to plants and/or animals when they come to the end of their life span. (By this time most children will be able to tell you that they become soil or decompose.)

4. Ask if anyone knows what helps animals or plants decompose. Encourage group discussion, because some child may have seen fungi growing on a log during your walks.

5. Bring out your branch, and ask for a description of the fungus. Ask what color plants have that this does *not* have. (Green) Ask if it can make its own food. (It cannot, because it lacks chlorophyll.)

   Ask where a fungus gets its food. (The fungus dissolves the branch, thus breaking the mole-cules down into small sugar molecules.)

6. How did the fungus know where the dead branch was? Does any-one remember seeing mush-rooms marching or fungi flying around looking for dead things to eat? How does fungus get to the proper place so it can grow?

Procedure

Part 1

1. Distribute a data sheet with a spore print to each group. Ask the children where the mush-room cap-shaped picture came from. Why is it so smudgy? Why does the picture have the same pattern as the gills?

   Have the children use hand lenses to notice that the smudges are made of particles so small, they can't be seen individually.

2. Throw up a handful of samara seeds, and ask what they are for. (For trees to continue their life cycles.) How do samaras get around? (Wind) What part of a plant makes seeds? (Flowers)

3. Refer the children back to the print. What do they think came from the mushroom to make the print? Allow group sharing and someone will excitedly realize that these smudges are "seeds" from the mushroom.

   Explain that these are too small to be called seeds, so they are called spores, but they have the same job as seeds. (Allow for group discussion and sharing.)

4. Does anyone now know why you don't see mushrooms or fungi traveling through the woods and landing on dead objects?

   Allow time for group dis-cussion and the writing of hypotheses.

5. Explain that the children are going to test the idea that fungus spores are flying all around by recreating the conditions they can grow in.

   "Dead bread" will serve as a model for dead logs. Why will the children add water and place the bread in a dark place? (The water simulates rain, while the darkened area simulates the shady forest.)

6. Each group will select a place to gather these invisible spores. One group may pat the bread upon their sneaker soles, another may touch the bread to the floor, or pat it on some plant soil, or rub it on a window sill. Ask one group to simply wave the bread in the air, just in case fungus spores are flying there!

7. The children should complete Observation 1 by drawing the bread as it appears in the bag, and by writing a statement about how it still looks like bread.

   Each group should tape its label to the bag before handing it to you for placement in the "shady" closet.

8. End your lesson here by asking for predictions of what the "dead bread" will look like after a few days.

Part 2

9. After several days, you will observe great changes in the bread, so it is time to hand out the bags to each group. Caution them not to open the bags. (They may not even want to touch the bags!)

10. Give time for writing of statements describing what the "dead bread" looks like now.

11. Acceptable conclusion answers: 1. spores; 2. spores, life cycle; 3. decomposer.

12. You may want to mention that bacterial colonies may have also begun to grow upon the bread, as decomposers.

    Where did the bacteria come from? Why is it important to wash your hands before you eat?

To Think About

You may want to ask children, (after they finished the lesson) where would food 'keep' better: the rainforest or the North Pole? Why? If I want my food to stay in good condition I should keep it: _____ .

 **Connections**

- **Science:** The Friendly Fungus Physical Factors! followup (page 56) is designed to help your ecologists realize that certain environmental conditions must be present in order for organisms to thrive. You may assign it as homework or, if there is a refrigerator available at your school, as class work.

  Use this lesson to explain why food must be taken care of properly to avoid waste and illness.

  Conclusion answers: 1. in the warm bag; 2. Antarctica.

- **Social Studies:** Research how people preserved their food before the advent of the refrigerator.

- **Reading:**

  Seeds: Pop, Stick, Glide, Patricia Lauber. Crown, New York, 1981 (2–5).

  Chains, Webs and Pyramids: The Flow of Energy in Nature, Laurence Pringle. Harper, New York, 1975 (4–7).

  Plants Without Seeds, Helen J. Challand. Children's Press, Chicago, 1986 (2–4).

  Mushrooms and Molds, Robert Froman. Harper, New York, 1972 (1–3).

Fungus and Mushrooms!

Draw the underside of the mushroom cap here.	Draw what you found under the mushroom cap here.

What do you notice about your drawings?

▲ **PROBLEM:** How does fungus get to the dead things it decomposes? OR do mushrooms march and fungi fly?

■ **HYPOTHESIS:** _____

● **METHOD:**

OBSERVATIONS:
(Draw and write a statement.)

1. Pat bread on _____. "Rain" on it with water. Seal it in a bag and label it.

1. _____

2. Place in "shade" for several days. Keep it in the bag and observe it.

2. _____

★ **CONCLUSION:**

1. Fungus doesn't fly, but its _____ travel everywhere.

2. If the tiny _____ land on something dead, and they

   get enough rain, they will continue the _____ of a fungus, the way seeds do for green plants.

3. Fungus must be a _____ because they do not have chlorophyll to make their own food.

Friendly Fungus Physical Factors! (Followup)

▲ **PROBLEM:** Where will fungus spores grow better—in cold places or warm places?

■ **HYPOTHESIS:** _____

_____

● **METHOD:**

1. Take 2 small pieces of bread of equal size. Place them in 2 small plastic bags.

   Put 10 ml or 2 teaspoons of water into each bag. Seal.

   After you sketch them in Observation 1, place one bag in the freezer, and the other in a dark place.

2. After 7 days, look at the bread in both bags. Draw them in Observation 2. Write a statement about each.

   Don't open bags after you put bread in!

☞ **OBSERVATIONS:**

1.

Warm Bag	Cold Bag

2.

Warm Bag	Cold Bag

_____

_____

★ **CONCLUSION:**

1. The fungus spores grew better _____.
2. This probably means dead things take a very long time to

   decompose in _____.

Food Web Crossword Game

Creating and playing the Food Web Crossword Game will afford your students both research and cooperative planning opportunities and give them practice in these . . .

Science Skills
1. *Observation*
2. *Sequencing*
3. *Research*, in this case to find information which will form the basis of the game.

Cooperative Group Management

Be sure that weaker students are placed with at least one strong researcher who knows his/her way around the library or encyclopedia.

A student who is terrific in art may be appointed the group artist, while another student might be great at lettering the cards.

Everyone should research at least one chain. More able students can research more than one chain.

Materials Needed

1. Food chain card sets which children have researched and drawn upon copies of the blank cards on page 59. (Make at least one copy for each child, with several extras for those who research long chains.)
2. Several boxes to contain the cards. Be sure they are large enough for you to tape the rules and answers onto the bottom of the lid.

✔ Getting Started

1. After you review food chains, ask what a spider weaves, or what another name for a word map is. (Web.)

   Ask what the children think two or more food chains woven together are called. (A food web.)

   Explain that most food chains do not exist by themselves but are connected into webs. You might want to draw examples of food webs upon the board (see the diagram on page 58).
2. Each group will select a continent or region of the Earth.
3. Each member of the group will be responsible for choosing a secondary or tertiary consumer to research and trace its food chain. For example, if the group chooses Africa, a child may choose lions to research.

   The more chains that are researched, the better the game will be.
4. When the child has traced back to the producer in the lion's food chain, he/she may begin transferring that information to the blank cards provided. (Since books which give information on animals and their food are unlikely to mention decomposers, these are provided on the sample cards.)
5. The information on the card must include where the organism ranks in the food chain as a producer, a primary, secondary, or tertiary consumer, or a decomposer.

   Vocabulary such as *herbivore,*

carnivore, scavenger, or *omnivore* must also be included on the type of eater line.

To ensure that players know which cards belong to which chain, each group should cooperatively choose a symbol and place it in the box at the bottom right of each of their cards.

6. After you check the cards, laminate them and cut them apart.

7. Place cards from different areas into separate boxes, so you end up with several games the children can rotate.

Depending on the number of cards in each box, two to four children can play with each deck.

Paste the following on each box:

Object of the Game
To assemble a food chain and link it to others to form a "crossword" food web.

How to Play
1. Mix up the cards and place them in a deck face down between the players.

2. The dealer gives four cards face down to each player.

3. Look at your cards. You are trying to build up a complete food chain.

Most of the cards have the name of a plant or animal and a symbol in the bottom right corner. All the cards in a chain have the same symbol.

4. The last person to receive cards is the first one to draw a card. The card may be kept (for example, if it belongs to the same food chain as one of the dealt cards).

Any unwanted card may be discarded, face down. In later turns, players may keep up to 6 cards in their hand.

5. The turn to draw a card then passes to the player on the left, and continues to pass around until the end of the game.

6. The first player who thinks he/she has a complete food chain says, "Food Chain" and displays the cards in order (either from decomposer down to producer or producer up to decomposer). The player receives 1 point and is then dealt four replacement cards.

7. Players have a right to challenge if they believe that the person naming the food chain has done so incorrectly. If the challenge is correct, the challenger is awarded 1 point. Incorrect challenges get a negative point.

8. The next player who finds a complete food chain may also lay his/her cards upon the table. The player should try to connect the chain, crossword fashion, with a chain already on the table.

To do this, one of the cards in his/her chain must either be the same as a card in the chain on the table *or* represent the same link in that chain. For example, with a chain containing "leaf," that card could be placed over the "algae" card in the diagram, since many insects eat leaves.

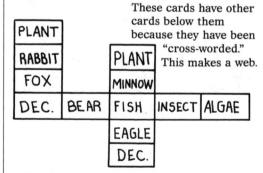

These cards have other cards below them because they have been "cross-worded." This makes a web.

If the player makes this crossword connection, he/she receives *2 points* and is then dealt four cards.

How to Win
The player with the highest number of points when all the cards have been used up *or* when time is up is the winner.

Food Web Crossword Blanks

1. I have agreed to research the food chain of a _____.

2. The area our food chains come from is _____.

3. The labeled, colored cards are due _____.

4. I know that every food chain must have a producer, consumer(s) and a decomposer. (Note this on line that says position in food chain.)

5. The decomposer card has already been drawn for me, so all I have to do for that one is fill in the symbol box. Only cards in my food chain will have this symbol.

Decomposer	
Position in Food Chain Earthworm and Bacteria · Fungus — Fungus mainly decompose plants. Bacteria, worms and some insects decompose anything dead. — **Type of "vore"** [ ]	**Position in food chain** — **Type of "vore" or producer or scavenger** [ ]
Position in Food Chain — **Type of "vore" or producer or scavenger** [ ]	**Position in food chain** — **Type of "vore" or producer or scavenger** [ ]

Plunge into Plant Chemistry
Nutritional Co-op: Classified Info (Followup)
Finding Fat in Food (Followup)

Recommended for Grades 3 and Up

Using simple chemical tests in two 30-minute lessons will allow your chemists to understand how nutrients in a plant can help it continue its life span and life cycle. Children will also understand these . . .

Science Concepts

1. Living things have adaptations for survival and for the continuation of their life cycle.
2. Green plants begin food chains because they can perform photosynthesis.
3. Plants and animals depend on each other in a community.
4. The interaction of two substances may change their form and create a system.

Why Teach This?

My students' eyes light up when they perform investigations utilizing chemistry. This attitude makes it very easy to slip in a review of the function of plant parts and how they interact with each other, animals, and the Earth in an ecosystem.

Chemical analysis of nutrients is a terrific springboard to a unit on proper nutrition. (See the followups in the Connections section.)

This is also an excellent opportunity to teach children to keep their hands away from their faces, especially in a chemistry experiment, and to show that chemicals are safe if they are handled properly.

Cooperative Group Management

Since there are four specific tasks in each nutrient testing section, it is convenient to arrange equipment for groups of two or four.

Groups of two or four also make it easy for the children to review their group notes and plant word maps from Leaf It to Chromatography (page 34) and their Mini-Weed Guide (page 44) for background information in completing both the hypothesis and conclusion sections of the data sheets.

Materials Needed

1. A source of heat for the water. (An electric coffeepot is great.)
2. A clear pyrex bowl or pot for the hot water.
3. An oven mitt or tongs for handling the heated test tubes.

For each group

4. A paper plate.
5. Two tiny chunks of apple, pear, peach, or other sweet fruit (about one cubic cm).
6. Two or three green peas or corn kernels. (Use frozen to avoid wasting the leftovers.)
7. Two tiny bits of lettuce (about one square cm).
8. Two tiny chunks of white or sweet potato.
9. A dropper bottle with dilute iodine. (Iodine is **poisonous** if ingested and will stain clothing,

so dilute it with water until it is a pale brown.)

10. A dropper bottle with Benedict's solution. (You can obtain this either from your local high school or from a science supply company—a bottle is inexpensive and will last for years. Benedict's solution is not harmful to the skin, but must be handled carefully and **not ingested.**)

11. Four test tubes with rack or holder. (I find that the sight of test tubes is a terrific motivator. If you can't purchase them, try your local junior or high school.)

12. A paper towel for spills.

For each child

13. Data sheets.

✓ Getting Started

1. Ask what it means to have a nutritious meal. What is a nutrient? Ask if anyone ever reads the cereal box in the morning. What words can they remember from the list of nutrients?

2. Allow time for the groups to discuss this and representative share.

    You may wish to list some of the nutrients they should be able to come up with. Protein, carbohydrate, and fat are nutrients which offer caloric value for growth and energy, while vitamins and minerals do not provide calories but enable the body to use the calories properly.

    Explain that the nutrient carbohydrate may be found in two basic forms: sugar and starch. You may wish to explain that starch is produced when sugar molecules join together to make a larger, more complex molecule. This is where the term *complex carbohydrate* comes from.

3. Have the children group review their prior plant information in Leaf it to Chromatography (page 34) and Weed Wonders (page 43).

    Before they write their hypothesis, ask what two nutrients they would most expect to find in a plant, if the plant's leaves manufacture sugar and sugar molecules can be combined to make starch.

Procedure

Part 1

1. Direct the chemists' attention to the first data sheet page which says: Chemical Tests To Know About: **Indicators.**

    Ask if someone can indicate what color shirt you are wearing. Ask for a definition of indicator. (Something that tells or informs.)

    Hold up an iodine bottle (the color of the liquid should be visible) and ask how iodine will indicate that part of a plant has starch in it. (The iodine will turn black.)

2. Have the children draw lines to divide the paper plates into four sections, and then label each section with what is being tested—fruit, seed, leaf, and root or tuber. Then have them place one piece of each plant part in its section.

3. Discuss the importance of handling the iodine properly, and not sampling any of the foods during or after the testing with iodine.

    Note: Only you or another adult should dispense iodine.

    Place two drops of iodine on a different plant part. After each test, the child should write his/ her observation of what the iodine did.

4. You may wish to emphasize that an observation should mention **only** what the children see. Thus they should not mention that starch is present because they can't see the starch itself.

Part 2

5. Review the chemical indicator test for sugar.

   Ask what color Benedict's solution will turn if there is a little sugar in a food. (Green or yellow, as compared to brick red, if there is a lot.)

6. Heat up your water to near boiling and allow the children to place their second bits of plant parts into the test tubes. Then have each group place 12 to 15 drops of Benedict's solution into the tubes (i.e., each child gets to place 3 to 5 drops).

7. You may wish to have the children label the tubes holding potato or apple so they can tell the difference.

   Place the tubes into the bowl of hot water and allow time for the reactions to occur.

8. This provides a few moments to both review Observations 1 through 4 and write Conclusion 1. (Starch will be found in the seed and the potato [tuber] or sweet potato [root]. Traces may be found under the skin of an apple.)

9. By this time the Benedict's solution should have reacted. Hold up each test tube (with mitt or tongs) so the children can write their observations and then proceed to Conclusion 2. (The most sugar will be found in the fruit, with some in the root or tuber and possibly some in the seed— especially if you used green peas.) The leaf should show lit-

tle reaction. Don't be tricked by the green of the leaf showing through the beautiful peacock blue shade of the Benedict's.)

10. Conclusion 3 asks the children to connect *life cycles* to the idea that if fruits have the nutrient *sugar* animals will *eat them* and drop the seeds with their waste products.

    Conclusion 4 states that embryo plants in seeds need *starch or sugar or nutrients* to survive (while they are unable to perform photosynthesis).

    Conclusion 5 states that green leaves perform photosynthesis to make sugar, and send the extra sugar to the root or tuber bank for rainy days and the beginning of spring when buds are too small to make sugar.

Connections

- **Nutrition:** Use the Nutrition Co-op: Classified Info! followup (page 66). Set up a nutrition information cooperative exchange by having the children bring in labels from processed foods. They should then use the followup sheet both to practice reading labels and to classify foods into the newly designed Nutrition Pyramid the federal government has established.

  Continue your exploration of nutrients by using the Finding Fat in Food followup (page 67).

- **Research and Chart Making:** What vitamins and minerals are necessary for good nutrition? What foods provide them? List the major vitamins and minerals and assign each group to research a different selection. Have the groups report their information so a class chart can be compiled.

- **Mathematics:** Design nutritious menus and have the children calculate how many calories each meal contains. (They can use information on food packages, or you might buy an inexpensive calorie counting book.)

  Play the Edible Plants Venn Diagram Game in *Dirt Cheap Science* (Scholastic, 1992).

- **Social Studies:** Have the children compare and contrast the diets of the cultural groups you are studying with their own diets.

- **Reading**
  A Book of Vegetables, Harriet Langsam Sobol. Putnam, New York, 1984 (3–5).

  Potatoes, Sylvia A. Johnson. Lerner, Minneapolis, 1984 (4–7).

  Foodworks, Ontario Science Centre. Addison Wesley, Redding, MA. 1990 (3–7).

  Write to the Human Nutrition Information Service, Room 325, 6505 Belcrest Road, Hyattville, MD 20782, for more information on the 29-page Food Guide Pyramid booklet.

Plant Chemistry

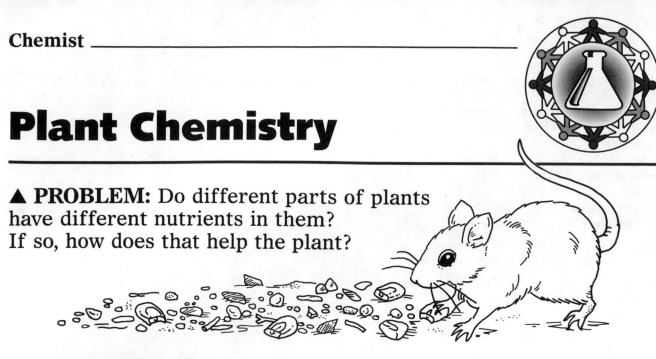

▲ **PROBLEM:** Do different parts of plants have different nutrients in them? If so, how does that help the plant?

■ **HYPOTHESIS:** _____

_____

Chemical Tests To Know About: Indicators!

  ***Iodine** *turns black to indicate the* nutrient starch.
****Benedict's solution** *turns from blue to green to yellow to brick red to indicate the* nutrient sugar *when placed in a hot water bath.*

● **METHOD:**

1. Place fruit on plate. Drop 2 drops of iodine* on it.

2. Repeat as above with peeled or split seed.

3. Repeat as above with leaf.

4. Repeat with root or tuber. (potato)

👁 **OBSERVATIONS:**

1. The iodine _____

   _____

2. _____

3. _____

4. _____

5. Place fruit into test tube. Place 12 drops of Benedict's Solution** into it. Place in hot water bath. Wait and watch.

5. The Benedict's Solution

_____

_____

_____

6. Repeat as in (5) with peeled seed.

6. _____

_____

7. Repeat as in (5) with leaf.

7. _____

_____

8. Repeat as in (5) with root or tuber.

8. _____

_____

★ CONCLUSION:

1. The parts of plants that had the nutrient starch were

_____

2. The parts of plants that had the nutrient sugar were

_____

3. Seeds have to be dispersed to continue their _____

_____, so maybe fruits have the nutrient _____

so animals will _____ and drop the seeds with their waste products.

4. Embryo plants in seeds need _____ to survive.

5. Green leaves perform _____ to make sugar and

send the extra sugar to the _____ bank for rainy

days and the beginning of _____ when buds are too small to make sugar.

Nutrition Co-op: Classified Info!

*This is the new U.S.D.A. Nutrition Pyramid. It shows how many daily servings you should have from each food group.

1. Which group should you eat the most of?

_____

2. What is the lowest total number of vegetable and fruit servings you should have each day?

_____

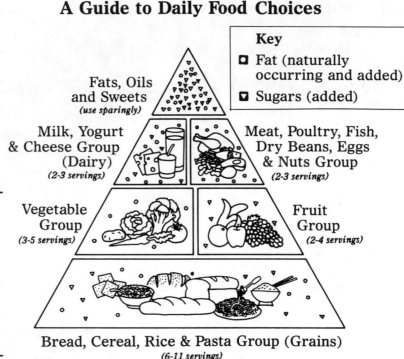

A Guide to Daily Food Choices

Key
◻ Fat (naturally occurring and added)
◻ Sugars (added)

Fats, Oils and Sweets *(use sparingly)*

Milk, Yogurt & Cheese Group (Dairy) *(2-3 servings)*

Meat, Poultry, Fish, Dry Beans, Eggs & Nuts Group *(2-3 servings)*

Vegetable Group *(3-5 servings)*

Fruit Group *(2-4 servings)*

Bread, Cereal, Rice & Pasta Group (Grains) *(6-11 servings)*

3. Which food group should you eat the least of? _____

★**ACTIVITY 1** Bring 5 labels in from canned, boxed, or frozen foods. Classify them into a large pyramid your group draws on a large sheet of paper. If the food has more than 5 grams of fat per serving, be sure to count that as a serving in the Fat Section.

★★**ACTIVITY 2** Write a menu for a full day showing what you would choose for breakfast, lunch, dinner and snacks. Include the minimum number of servings for each classification of foods.

*__To use the pyramid,__ count a serving from the grain group as 1 slice of bread, 1 ounce of cereal or $\frac{1}{2}$ cup of pasta or rice. Vegetable and fruit servings generally are $\frac{1}{2}$ cup sizes, or medium sized apples, bananas, or oranges. One cup of leafy greens is one serving.
• Dairy servings are 1 cup of milk or yogurt or $1\frac{1}{2}$–2 ounces of cheese.
• Meat servings should not be more than 5–7 ounces cooked.
• One egg or 2 tablespoons of peanut butter count as 1 oz. of meat.
• Most meat and dairy products have fat, so don't forget to count that for your fat category.

Home Investigation: Finding Fat in Food

Have some fun finding out how healthy some of the foods you eat really are! Your diet should not include foods high in fat on a regular basis. Here's how to test for fat in food:

1. Cut out a brown paper bag to get a section that measures 30 cm by 30 cm.

2. Fold the bag into eight sections, so you can test eight foods. Number the boxes 1–8.

3. Write the name of each food in the numbered boxes on this sheet. Then rub a little of each food in the matching section of brown paper.

4. Wait a half hour to let moisture (water) from the food, evaporate. Then hold the brown paper up to the light.

5. If light shines through a section, the food has fat.

6. Fill out this sheet with your observations and conclusion.

Name of Food	Fat?	Name of Food	Fat?
1.		5.	
2.		6.	
3.		7.	
4.		8.	

★ **CONCLUSION:** I will limit my eating of _____

because _____

Metamorphosis Magic

Long term observations of a butterfly's life cycle, with several mini-lessons, will lead your entomologists delightedly to these . . .

Science Concepts

1. Animals have adaptations which enable them to survive in their environment.
2. Animals go through a series of changes from egg to the adult stage which is capable of producing the next generation. This series of changes is called the life cycle.
3. Many types of animals do not depend upon the adult parent to care for them during their immature stages.
4. Plants and animals depend upon each other in a community.

Why Teach This?

Studying butterflies is a delightful way to introduce insects, which may have negative overtones for some of your students (and even you!).

Insects and flowering plants have a close relationship as pollinators and as providers of food thus offering a great living example of the interdependence of plants and animals.

Cooperative Group Management

Each child should be responsible for making daily observations and recordings of the progress of the life cycle of the butterfly you select.

Four to eight children can easily share one larva in a cup for observation purposes. When the larvae arrive, you may wish to divide the tasks enumerated in the Getting Started section among the group members.

Materials Needed

1. Several butterfly larvae along with an easily assembled box for viewing and a food supply. (All of this can be ordered as a set from a science supply company. Painted lady larvae are inexpensive and take a relatively short time to pupate and emerge as adults.)

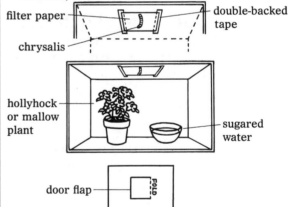

2. A soft paintbrush.
3. Two 3-inch flower pots with soil.
   b. A package of hollyhock seeds.

For each group
4. A small plastic cup.
5. A coffee filter cut to cover the cup.
6. A rubber band to fit around the cup.
7. Masking tape.

For each child
8. Data sheets.

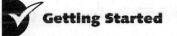

Getting Started

1. The small pots will fit into the butterfly box to provide a plant for the adult butterflies to lay their eggs on.

2. Explain that some special guests are coming to the class and will need the plants for a very special reason. Encourage group discussion with class representation as to what type of living thing this could possibly be.

3. When the larvae arrive, place a small quantity of the feeding medium (usually mashed mallow or hollyhock leaves) into each group's cup.

    Using a soft paintbrush, gently brush each caterpillar into a cup. Cover the cups with the filter paper and fasten them down with the rubber band. (If there is a hole punched in the filter, be sure it is not in a place where the caterpillar can make a run for it!)

Procedure

1. Have the children begin the Part 1 data sheet by writing their predictions about their group's "visitor."

2. Of course, many of the children will know that their visitor is a caterpillar, but ask if anyone knows what a caterpillar really is. (A larva or immature form of insect.)

    Explain that each day, everyone will be responsible for keeping track of the visitor.

3. Encourage a complete description of the caterpillar, including its size in the Day One Observation section.

    Children can use the paper ruler to measure the caterpillar in the cup, without removing amd possibly harming it. They

can fold the ruler and place it alongside the larva.

   Wherever you choose to place the caterpillars in your room, **be sure they are not sitting on a window sill or you will have cooked critters.** (The same goes for your butterfly box.)

5. When the caterpillars reach the chrysalis stage, they will fasten themselves to the filter paper. (A chrysalis is the hardened skin of the larva.)

    Double back some masking tape onto the top of your butterfly box, and gently press the filter paper to it.

6. After several days, depending upon the temperature of your room, the chrysalises will begin to gently twitch as they hang down. They will become slightly translucent, and then the amazing transformation will become apparent as the butterflies start to emerge.

    A reddish fluid called meconium will stain the floor of the butterfly box. The butterfly releases this fluid when it pumps its wings. Don't expect it to fly until the wings dry out.

7. Place some sugared water into a small shallow bowl, so the butterflies can feed. The children will be amazed to see the long drinking tube called a *proboscis* unfurl as the butterflies sip the sugar water.

    Discuss the following questions: Where would a butterfly find a sweet liquid like this outside? (Nectar from flowers.) Why do butterflies need such long strawlike jaws? (To reach inside the flower petals for the nectar.) What could get picked up by the butterfly as it sat upon a flower? (Pollen.)

8. Ask if anyone thinks the butterfly looks like the larva that

it used to be. Ask if anyone knows what big word is used to describe such a change. (Metamorphosis.)

Do people go through metamorphosis? How do you know they don't?

What is the advantage of metamorphosis? (It enables the species to use two different sources of food—plant leaves and nectar—and thus is an adaptation which increases the survival of the species.)

9. Encourage the children to look very closely at the adult butterfly's body. The painted lady butterfly may appear to have only four legs, but that is because its first pair of legs is held in a folded position near its body.

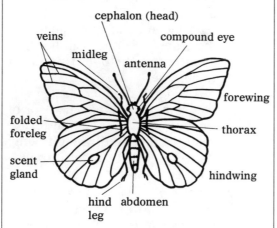

How many body sections does the butterfly have? How many wings? See the diagram so the children can properly label the body parts on their observation sketch.

10. If you have hollyhock plants with leaves, keep replenishing the sugar water supply so the butterflies can continue to feed. If you are lucky, some butterflies may lay eggs upon the leaves after they mate.

11. Even if you don't continue with the plants, discuss the fact that the butterflies do not have live babies but lay eggs upon leaves. Ask why. (When the tiny caterpillars hatch, they do not have to look for food. That is the total extent of the care given by a mother butterfly to its young.)

Why are so many eggs laid? (Most are eaten by ants and some spiders, or destroyed by smaller insects which lay their eggs inside the butterfly eggs. When the insect's larvae hatch, they eat the butterfly eggs.)

12. Have the children complete the Part 2 data sheet. Answers: 1. leaves (may vary); 2. sugared water, tongue; 3. flower, bird (may vary); 3a. life; 4. metamorphosis; 5. (varies); 6. to lay eggs on; 7. food for the baby caterpillars; 8. life cycle.

- **Mathematics:** The children will be amazed at how quickly the larvae grow. They might want to calculate how big they would be if they grew at the same rate in the same time.

Let the beauty of a butterfly's wings launch an investigation into symmetry.

- **Reading:**
Butterflies and Moths, James P. Rowan. Children's Press, Chicago, 1982 (1–4).

Terry and the Caterpillars, Millicent E. Selsam. Harper, New York, 1962 (K–3).

A First Look at Caterpillars, Millicent E. Selsam and Joyce Hunt. Walker, New York, 1988 (1–3).

Butterfly and Moth, Paul Whalley. Knopf, New York, 1988 (4–8).

Metamorphosis Magic: Part I—Now!

1. Predict and explain what classroom guests are coming and tell why you think they need plants.

_____

_____

2. Describe your guest, measure it, and keep track of any changes you notice over the next several days. Sketch your guest every time something new happens.

Date:	Date:
Date:	Date:
Date:	Date:
Date:	Date:

Cut this paper ruler out. Gently place it near your guest. Fold it back if necessary so it fits in the cup.

1 2 3 4 5 6 7 8 9 10 11 12

Metamorphosis Magic: Part II—Wow!

1. What did your guest eat while it was a caterpillar?

   _____

2. What does the adult butterfly eat? How does it get the food into

   its body? _____

3. What do you think a good source of food would be for a
   butterfly that was outdoors? What animal might have butterflies

   in its food chain? _____

AHA! What cycle could butterflies help plants with? _____

4. Were you surprised by the big change the butterfly went

   through? What is this change called? _____

5. **Look** very carefully at the adult
   butterfly. Sketch it with the correct
   number of body sections, legs, wings,
   and head (cephalon) adaptations.
   Label what you can.

6. Why did the adult female butterfly need plants?

   _____

7. What do you think the plants will be used for next?

   _____

8. What cycle does metamorphosis take place in?

   _____   _____

Arthropod Hunt: A "Joint" Exploration

Classroom observations, followed by a school grounds tour, add up to two 40-minute lessons that will empower your entomologists to discover various six- and eight-legged creatures along with these . . .

Science Concepts

1. Animals have adaptations which enable them to survive in their environment.
2. The behavior of an animal may be instinctive or inborn rather than taught.
3. The number of animals of a particular type in a defined area is known as a *population*.
4. Plants and animals depend upon each other in a community.

Why Teach This?

Besides serving as pollinators, insects play a vital role as decomposers, and are found in the food chains and webs of many animals.

Understanding the role that insects and spiders play on Earth will help your children gain an appreciation for these creatures that many people see in a negative light—and also for the complexity and delicate balance of the ecosystem.

Cooperative Group Management

For a schoolwide arthropod hunt, teams of two tend to work best. The teams can pair up to exchange information about what they found.

Representative Sharing for a class survey should follow this activity.

If you have no schoolyard where insects are likely to be found, try to schedule a trip to a nearby park. Or you might assign this exploration as a homework activity with a long lead time, so children can visit parks with their parents and share their discoveries with the class.

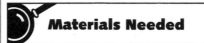
Materials Needed

1. Plastic petri dishes for specimen collection.
2. Tape to seal the dishes.

For each group
3. Crayons.

For each child
4. Data sheets.

Getting Started

1. This lesson is best taught during the late spring, when your children are getting "antsy" and the likelihood of insects being about is increased.

Throughout the year, anytime you or a child find a dead insect or spider, scoop it into a plastic petri dish. Cover the dish and seal it so the insect does not fall out. If you find molts (exoskeletons or shells of cicadas clinging to tree trunks or wooden objects) collect them too.

The advantage of a petri dish collection of insects and spiders is that it provides a nonthreatening way for children to view animals they might normally be leery of. They can also view the top and bottom of the arthropod without handling it and breaking it.

Procedure

Part 1

1. Tell the children they are going on an arthropod hunt around the school, but first they need to discover what an arthropod is.

2. Hand out several insects and spiders in their dishes, rotate them through the class, and challenge the groups to compare one specimen to another, listing as many similarities as possible.

   No matter what insects or spiders you have in the collection, they will all have jointed legs and hard outer shells. Ask if anyone has ever heard of the joint disease called *arthritis*. If the suffix *pod* means foot or feet, does anyone now know what an arthropod is? Make sure the children understand that an arthropod is an animal with jointed legs or feet and an outer shell.

   Allow time for the hypothesis on Arthropod Hunt, Part 1.

3. To help the children discover what the hard shell really is, have the children examine cicada shells or molts to notice the little split that runs down the back of the thorax to the abdomen. This is where the insect wriggled out of its exoskeleton (shell).

   Ask if anyone has to get a new skeleton when they grow, and explain that arthropods do! They grow inside their hard skeletons, and when they get too big they slip out, much the same way children slip out of their clothing. Have the children feel their own backbones, and elicit that their backbones are internal, not external. Ask if anyone now knows what an exoskeleton is.

4. Ask the children to recall how many body parts a butterfly has, and then inform the children that they have a good clue for distinguishing between spiders and insects. Spiders have only two body parts—a *cephalothorax* (a combination head and thorax) and an *abdomen*.

   If you have beetles in your collection, be sure the children turn them over to observe that these have three main body sections.

5. Direct attention to the number of legs an insect has, and point out that this is another way to tell the difference. Spiders have eight legs, not six, all attached to the cephalothorax. In addition, spiders have neither wings nor antennae.

   Allow time for the completion of Data Sheet 1. Conclusion answers: spiders, insects (or the reverse), jointed legs and outer shell or exoskeleton. *Aha!* answer: outer shells or exoskeletons.

Part 2

6. Distribute Data Sheet 2 and explain that it is now time for the arthropod hunt. The children are to find arthropods, sketch them, and note where they were found, their colors, what their activity was, and what their population was in that area.

   Ask if the children anticipate it being easy to find an insect or spider. What adaptation could make it difficult? (Camouflage might help the arthropods blend into their background.)

   What adaptation could trick the children into thinking the insect or spider was something else? (Mimicry might make them think they were seeing a twig, for instance, when they were looking at an insect called a walking stick.)

   Caution the children not to

disturb any arthropods while observing them.

7. Outside, encourage children to look carefully at tree trunks, under dead logs, and at small mounds of dirt or sand (for ants). Be sure to encourage careful sketching, so the children note the number of body parts and legs for classification purposes.

   If the children observe arthropod activity, this is a good time to discuss instinctive behavior as opposed to learned behavior. For example, if you see a spider spinning a web, you might ask: Did the spider go to school to learn what it's doing? Did it learn that from its parents?

8. Even if no insects or spiders make an appearance, the children will find clues to their presence. For example, leaves with holes will show that insects were chewing a meal.

   The children should also note spider webs woven between branches as evidence of arthropod activity and plant and animal interaction.

9. Back in class, have the children work for another ten minutes refining their observations, using crayon to illustrate any camouflage or mimicry adaptations they saw.

10. Allow time (possibly another day) for groups to exchange papers so the children can see what they might have missed, and for Representative Sharing.

Connections

• **Science:** Have each group complete a word map after discussing the following questions:

   How are insects valuable to the environment? (They are part of food chains which include humans, they help plants continue their life cycles by pollinating them, and they act as decomposers to recycle nutrients.)

   Why is it necessary to understand the life cycle of insects? (This understanding can help control insect pests which carry disease or destroy crops, because insects may be more vulnerable at certain points of their cycles.)

   Research the question of how insects communicate with each other. Bee dancing and moth pheromones are fascinating examples of communication techniques.

   Research other differences between spiders and insects besides their highly observable features and life cycles.

• **Social Studies:** What peoples include insects in their diets? What types are eaten? How are they prepared?

• **Reading:**

Foodworks, Ontario Science Centre, Addison Wesley, Redding, MA, 1990 (3–7).

Insect Magic, Michael G. Emsley and Kjell B. Sandved, Viking, New York, 1978. (The text is for adults, but the magnificent photographs of insects will fascinate children of any age.)

Invertebrates, Lionel Bender. Gloucester, New York, 1988 (3–6).

Spiders, Lionel Bender. Gloucester, New York, 1988 (3–4).

Spider Magic, Dorothy Hinshaw Patent. Holiday, New York, 1982 (2–5).

Insects, Illa Podendorf. Watts, New York, 1985 (2–3).

Golden Guides—Butterflies and Moths, Insect Pests, Insects, Spiders and Their Kin. Golden Press, New York (all ages).

Arthropod Hunt: Part I

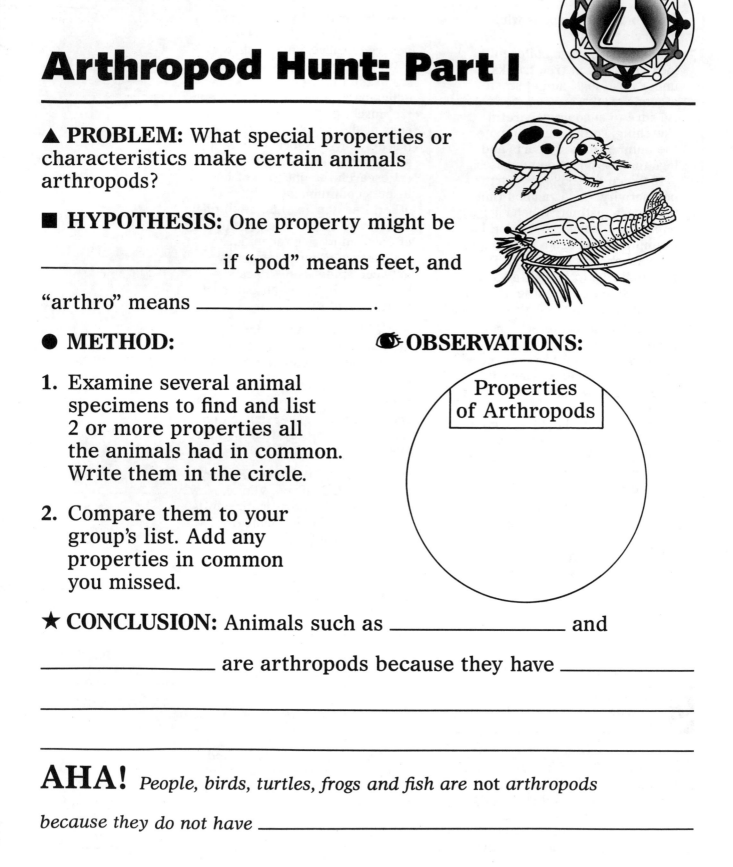

▲ **PROBLEM:** What special properties or characteristics make certain animals arthropods?

■ **HYPOTHESIS:** One property might be

_____ if "pod" means feet, and

"arthro" means _____.

● **METHOD:**

1. Examine several animal specimens to find and list 2 or more properties all the animals had in common. Write them in the circle.

2. Compare them to your group's list. Add any properties in common you missed.

👁 **OBSERVATIONS:**

Properties of Arthropods

★ **CONCLUSION:** Animals such as _____ and

_____ are arthropods because they have _____

_____

_____

AHA! *People, birds, turtles, frogs and fish are not arthropods*

because they do not have _____

_____

Arthropod Hunt: Part II

▲ **PROBLEM:** What helps arthropods survive near our school?

■ **HYPOTHESIS:** _____

_____

● **METHOD:** Sketch any arthropods you find. Tell where, what they were doing, and how many there were (population). Circle "insect" or "spider."

👁 **OBSERVATIONS: 1.**

Location Found	Sketch and Population of Each	Behavior
	Insect or Spider?　　Pop. ▢	
	Insect or Spider?　　Pop. ▢	
	Insect or Spider?　　Pop. ▢	

●● **METHOD: 2.** If you didn't see any arthropods, did you see any evidence that they were there?

👁👁 **OBSERVATIONS: 2.** _____

★ **CONCLUSION:** Arthropods near school could survive because

_____

What's My Rule? A Classification Game

You will not be able to get your students to stop analyzing buttons in a fascinating 20-minute to hour-long game, which teaches two important . . .

Science Concepts

1. *Observation* of an object or activity. This involves using one's senses (to see, hear, feel, smell, or taste, as appropriate) without imposing prior beliefs.
2. *Classification* of objects. This is based on observable properties such as size, shape, color, texture, odor, or taste as opposed to qualitative opinions.

Why Teach This?

Observation and classification are vital skills for organizing information in all fields of learning.

Cooperative Group Management

This game is best handled in groups of two. If you use the computer variation offered in the Connections section, you may have two children work with a database program and then invite a larger group of up to four more children to participate.

Materials Needed

1. A 5-pound bag of buttons. (You may buy this inexpensively at a crafts store—or you may ask for button donations from your class.)

For each group
2. A container that will hold five fistfuls of buttons.

For each child
3. Data sheet.

Getting Started

1. Write the words "The Not Game" on the board. Then call up several children, placing them into two groups based upon an observable property, such as boys and girls or red shirts and other shirts. Ask if anyone can guess your rule for placing them in the groups.

    If anyone says, "These are girls and the other group is boys," ask if they can restate the rule by using the word "not." They should be able to answer, "This group has girls, and this group does *not* have girls."

2. Practice this several times, making your groupings less easily identifiable—such as by sneakers tied and not tied. Invite children to write the rule for each grouping upon the board. Each set of rules must include the word "not."

    Hopefully, someone will come up with a qualitative rather than a quantitative rule, such as "These are wearing 'cool clothes' and those are not." Seize the opportunity to discuss the difference between observable fact and subjective opinion.

    In fact, if no one brings it up, make up a rule to illustrate why it is an incorrect classification technique (e.g. "These are happy and those are not").

 Procedure

1. Distribute the data sheets and a container of buttons to each group.
2. Expect excitement, so be sure to invite the children to look through your "special collection" before commencing the actual game.
3. Inform the children that they will be working with a partner to play What's My Rule? using buttons they must place into two groups.
4. Each child will take a fistful of buttons and place them on the table directly in front of him/her.

   Using all of the buttons from their fistful, the children must place them into two groups according to a rule based on observable properties. When they are satisfied with their rule, they must write it and its "not" part in sections 1A and 1B of their data sheet.
5. When the partners have both finished, they should turn to each other and say, "What's My Rule?"
6. Each partner has three tries to guess. After that the setter must show the correctly written rules to the guesser.
7. Be sure to circulate and check that the written rules are fair and objective and that the B section contains "not."
8. You may decide how many groupings the class is to make, and if the game is to be scored competitively.

   I find that the children are so motivated that they do not care about scoring. However, three points can be awarded if the rule is guessed upon the first try, two

points for the second, and one point for the third. If the guesser is stumped, the rule maker is awarded three points.
8. You may allow the children to take new fists of buttons for each rule or stay with the same fistful. (I feel that they are forced to think more creatively when they use the same buttons.)

Game Variation
1. The partners take turns grouping buttons. After one partner has completed grouping, the other should try to infer the rule and group his/her buttons accordingly.

   Then both children should write down their rules (or state them orally) and see if they agree. (No scoring is necessary.)

 **Connections**

- **Computer:** If you have access to a computer and a database program such as Bank Street Filer, two children may enter specific buttons into a database. (They merely have to follow the steps enumerated in the program.)

   Then the "computer experts" lay ten buttons, including the one filed into the database, in front of the keyboard. Several children can be invited to trace their way through the database to discover which button was entered.

Buttons which follow rule.

Not — Buttons which do not follow the rule.

- **Science:** See the classification games Ring Around the Plant World and Edible Plant Venn Diagram Game in *Dirt Cheap Science*.

   The next two lessons also deal with classification of animals.

What's Your Rule?
(A Classification System)

1a	2a	3a
1b	**2b**	**3b**

Magazine Safari or Where in the World?

In this activity, which requires at least three sessions, your zoologists will "travel" throughout the world as they research and create a classification game which will lead to these . . .

Science Concepts

1. Environmental conditions determine the type of animal populations which live within an area.
2. Different kinds of animals live in different environments.
3. Some animals migrate in order to meet their needs for survival. They may do this when physical factors in the environment change or when their needs change with a new stage in their life.

Why Teach This?

In addition to helping students understand the above concepts, the preparation and playing of this game also gives excellent practice in the skills of research and classifying.

Cooperative Group Management

The game has two stages requiring two different groups.

For preparing the cards, I find that teams of two work best. These teams will cut out illustrations from old magazines, paste them on pieces of paper, and label them. The children can divide these jobs according to their different abilities. (I feel it is better for the children to decide on the division, if possible.)

For playing the game, teams of four to eight work best. Although the children will naturally want their own team to win, emphasize the value of cooperation between teams. Explain that you will deduct points from any team making disparaging remarks about other teams.

Also point out that teams should watch other team placements carefully, because one team can benefit from another's mistake.

Materials Needed

1. A large stack of old *National Geographic, Nature,* or *Conservationist* magazines (You can ask parents for donations or see if the public library is discarding old magazines.)
2. A package of index cards.
3. Access to a laminating machine or clear contact paper to cover the cards.
4. Three 15-foot lengths of yarn, each a different color and tied at the ends to form three rings. Or three different colors of chalk, if you possess a large chalkboard. (See Procedure #1.)
5. (If you use the chalkboard:) Double stick tape or "gummy clay" for placing cards upon the board.

For each group
6. Markers or well sharpened crayons.
7. Six or more sheets of 8 × 11 in. tagboard or heavy white paper.
8. Scissors.

9. Glue sticks or white glue.

10. Data sheets. (Make as many copies as the number of cards you wish each group to prepare. See Getting Started #6.)

✔ Getting Started

1. Explain that the class is going to play a game called Magazine Safari, which they can also think of as a zoologist's version of "Where In The World?" But first the class has to create the game!

2. Hand out stacks of magazines to each group, and explain that the children are going to create game cards as they go on their magazine safari.

3. Each game card will have a picture of an animal, a label with its name on the front of the card, and some basic research information written on a data card and placed on the back.

4. The children will work in teams of two, researching, cutting, pasting, and creating the animal cards.

    The research should come from the article itself, if possible, so the children should try to answer the questions on the data cards before cutting up the magazine. If the information is not available, the children may use an encyclopedia to answer the questions on the data sheet.

5. After researching, one member of the team should cut out the animal and the other paste it upon heavyweight paper. The children can take turns labeling the animal cards and pasting the research card on the back of the paper.

6. Each team will be responsible for creating a minimum of six cards, so allot several class ses-

sions to the magazine safari itself.

7. You will need various Location Label cards. These are index cards with labels which you may either write yourself or assign to children, if some groups finish their research cards quickly.

    The labels must include LAND, AIR, and WATER. For advanced games you may want to add such labels as FOREST, DESERT, MOUNTAINS, RAIN FOREST, INTERTIDAL ZONE, FRESH WATER, SALT WATER, and other areas you may be studying. You may also want to have a set of cards with the names of the continents.

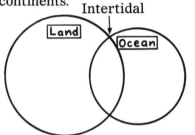

Use this for an oceanography unit.

8. Laminating the cards will increase the life of your game, and over the years you can build up an impressive card game supply.

---

1 2 3 Procedure

1. Place the three strings upon the floor or draw the three-ring Venn diagram upon the board.

2. Place the labels AIR, WATER, and LAND into the rings.

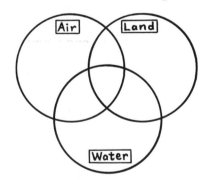

Discuss the intersections, and explain that an animal that spends time in two or all three regions should be placed in that particular intersection. For instance, a duck would be placed in the intersection of all three rings, because it flies, paddles, and nests upon the land.

3. For play, divide the class into several cooperative teams ranging in size from four to eight members, as nearly equal in number as possible.

   The team members should number off, starting with number one, so no one misses a turn as the team's spokesperson.

4. Inform the class that you will be selecting a card at random from the game box. The team that is up will confer to decide where the animal card should go in the Venn diagram. If the team places the card correctly, it receives a point.

5. If the card is correctly placed, the team may earn another point when you ask one bonus question from the research written on the back of the card. (The group may confer for the answers.)

   If the team gives an incorrect answer, its turn ends. There is no further penalty.

6. If the team does not correctly place the card, the next team has a chance to place it and answer questions.

Game Variations

1. To increase the difficulty of the game, substitute the other location cards or continent cards for the AIR, WATER, and LAND cards.

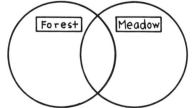

2. Increase the number of cards, to increase the information available.

Connections

- **Reading:**
  Animals and Where They Live, John Feltwell. Putnam, New York, 1988 (4–6).

  Secrets of Animal Survival, Donald J. Crump. National Geographic, Washington, DC, 1983 (4–8).

Magazine Safari Data Sheet

Paste on back of animal card

1. This animal's average life span is _____.

2. It can be classified as (circle one) an *invertebrate* or *vertebrate*. (If a vertebrate) the smaller group it belongs to is *fish, amphibian, reptile, bird* or *mammal*.

3. The animal *does* or *does not* take care of its young. (Circle one) If it does, this is how:

   _____

   _____

4. Draw as much of its food chain as you can:

5. This animal's enemy(enemies) are: _____

   _____

6. Some special adaptations are: _____

   _____

Paste label near animal or across it.

Animals in the Ring: A Venn Diagram Classification Game

Playing this game will help your enthusiastic zoologists master this . . .

Science Concept

1. Living things are classified in groups which are subsets of larger groups. Organisms in the subsets have the same properties or adaptations of the larger sets to which they belong.

Why Teach This?

Understanding classification of animals will help your students understand how scientists are able to organize the huge amounts of information they must deal with.

This game also provides painless practice in the skills of observation and chart reading, along with the satisfaction of being a cooperative team member.

Be sure to emphasize that the size of the set drawings in no way reflects the actual number of species which belong to it. For instance, the subset Arthropoda, which includes the insects, would have to take up the entire board to remotely reflect the vast array of insect species found on Earth.

Note that the invertebrate set is incomplete. I have included only those classes that children are most likely to be familiar with.

Cooperative Group Management

1. Divide the class into two teams. I usually find it easiest to use the natural division of back tables vs. front tables. It is not necessary to group according to ability.

2. Players help their teams by closely observing moves made by both teams and by knowing when it is their turn to come up without teacher invitation.

Emphasize that to be a cooperative team member also means refraining from offering any comments. These might distract the team from observing incorrect placements and remembering not to repeat them.

For the longer version, secretaries may be needed (see #2 under Longer Version).

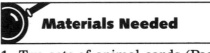
Materials Needed

1. Two sets of animal cards (Pages 90–96).
2. Access to a laminator or clear contact paper to protect the cards.
3. Colored chalks.
4. Double stick tape or "gummy wall clay."

For each group
5. (optional) A copy of the blank Venn diagram, if you wish your students to keep notes or if you play the longer version of the game.

Getting Started

1. After photocopying the two sets of cards, place a symbol such as a large dot on one set. (This will help you organize and reset the game quickly.) Then laminate or cover with contact paper.

2. Place a dotted and undotted set of animals upon the left and right edges of the board.

3. Sketch the Venn diagram outlines on the board, using a different color chalk for each subset near each other, to make it easier for the children to tell the lines apart.

   Be sure to sketch the subsets large enough so the animal cards can fit in. The cards can overlap, if necessary.

4. Place the labels into the proper subsets as shown on the Teacher's Venn Diagram sheet.

5. Inform the children that they are going to play a cooperative game which will help them organize animals into the special sets scientists have put them into.

   Emphasize that they do not have to know anything about the animals beforehand, because if they watch very carefully, they will learn a great deal by trial and error—mainly error at first!

Procedure

Short version

1. The first child on one team selects a card from the left side of the board and places it into a subset (using the tape or clay).

   Your job is merely to say "yes or no" depending upon the correctness of the placement.

   If the placement is correct, the next child on the same team gets to select a card and place it.

2. If the placement is incorrect, the other team is up.

   Caution the teams not to comment at any time during the game, because this means forfeiting a turn. This rule will enable your shyer students to come up without fear of possible ridicule for an incorrect placement.

   A turn is also forfeited if the person who is "it" does not come up to the board promptly. (This rule helps ensure that the children pay close attention throughout the game.)

3. The game continues until a team wins by placing all of its cards properly within the subsets.

Longer Version

1. Select the amount of time you wish the game to continue. I usually allot 15 minutes more for the longer game.

2. After properly placing a card, a team has the right to begin naming one or more properties or adaptations that each animal in the subset must possess in order to have been correctly classified. (See the Teacher's Data Sheet for possible properties.)

   I usually encourage each small team group within the larger team to work quietly together on a different subset, with a small team secretary. The teams then pool their information with representative sharings, with one child acting as the entire team's secretary. Information can be noted upon the student data sheet.

3. While this is occurring, the other team continues to place its cards. When they are all correctly placed, this team may begin its deliberations.

   At the time limit, the team which has the most information filled in on the secretary's student data sheet wins.

Connections

Reading:
All in the Family: Animal Species Around the World, Gilda Berger. Putnam, New York, 1981 (2–5).

Benny's Animals and How He Put Them in Order, Millicent E. Selsam. Harper, New York, 1966 (1–3).

Teacher's Data Sheet

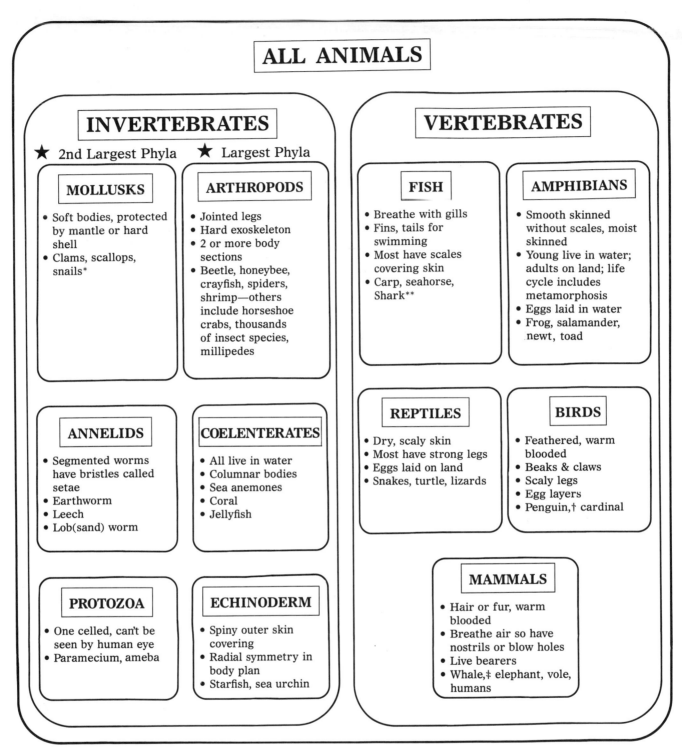

ALL ANIMALS

INVERTEBRATES

★ 2nd Largest Phyla   ★ Largest Phyla

MOLLUSKS
- Soft bodies, protected by mantle or hard shell
- Clams, scallops, snails*

ARTHROPODS
- Jointed legs
- Hard exoskeleton
- 2 or more body sections
- Beetle, honeybee, crayfish, spiders, shrimp—others include horseshoe crabs, thousands of insect species, millipedes

ANNELIDS
- Segmented worms have bristles called setae
- Earthworm
- Leech
- Lob(sand) worm

COELENTERATES
- All live in water
- Columnar bodies
- Sea anemones
- Coral
- Jellyfish

PROTOZOA
- One celled, can't be seen by human eye
- Paramecium, ameba

ECHINODERM
- Spiny outer skin covering
- Radial symmetry in body plan
- Starfish, sea urchin

VERTEBRATES

FISH
- Breathe with gills
- Fins, tails for swimming
- Most have scales covering skin
- Carp, seahorse, Shark**

AMPHIBIANS
- Smooth skinned without scales, moist skinned
- Young live in water; adults on land; life cycle includes metamorphosis
- Eggs laid in water
- Frog, salamander, newt, toad

REPTILES
- Dry, scaly skin
- Most have strong legs
- Eggs laid on land
- Snakes, turtle, lizards

BIRDS
- Feathered, warm blooded
- Beaks & claws
- Scaly legs
- Egg layers
- Penguin,† cardinal

MAMMALS
- Hair or fur, warm blooded
- Breathe air so have nostrils or blow holes
- Live bearers
- Whale,‡ elephant, vole, humans

★ **Reminder:** All phyla in Invertebrates are not shown.

*Note: octopus & squid are also mollusks
**Note: Sharks are a separate subset of fish due to their skeletons being made of cartilage.
† Note: Due to recognizable features, only 2 birds are pictured. Further note that penguins were chosen because some children may believe that they have fur, rather than down feathers.
‡ Note: Whale was chosen to allow for clarification of confusion—some children may believe they are fish.

Ring Around the Animals

★ **Reminder:** All groups of animals are not shown in the Invertebrates, and the size of the rings doesn't indicate size of group in real life.

All Animals

Invertebrates

Vertebrates

Fish	Amphibians
Reptiles	Birds
Mammals	Annelids
Arthropods	Mollusks
Coelenterates	Protozoa
Echinoderms	

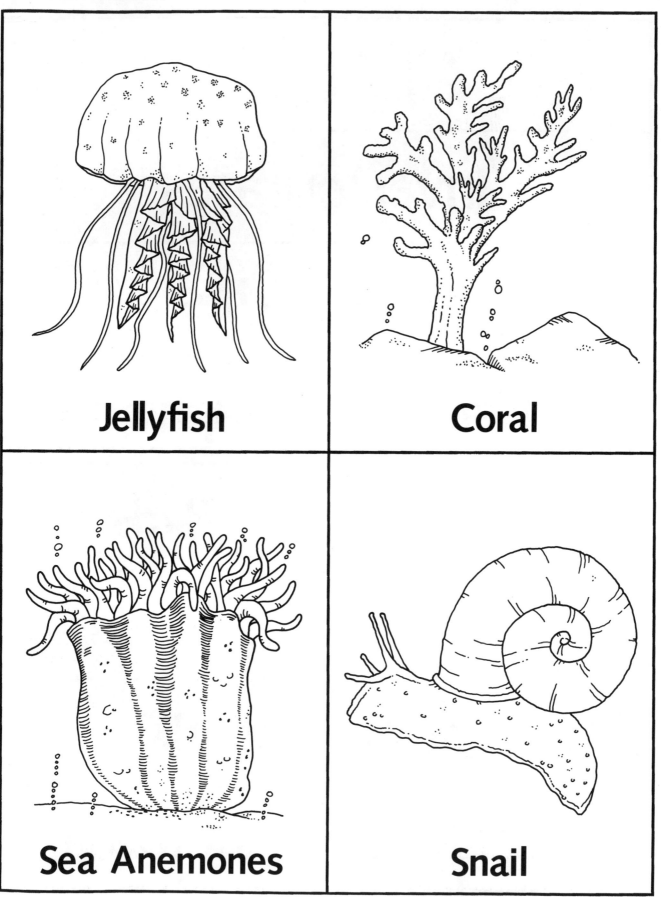

Jellyfish

Coral

Sea Anemones

Snail

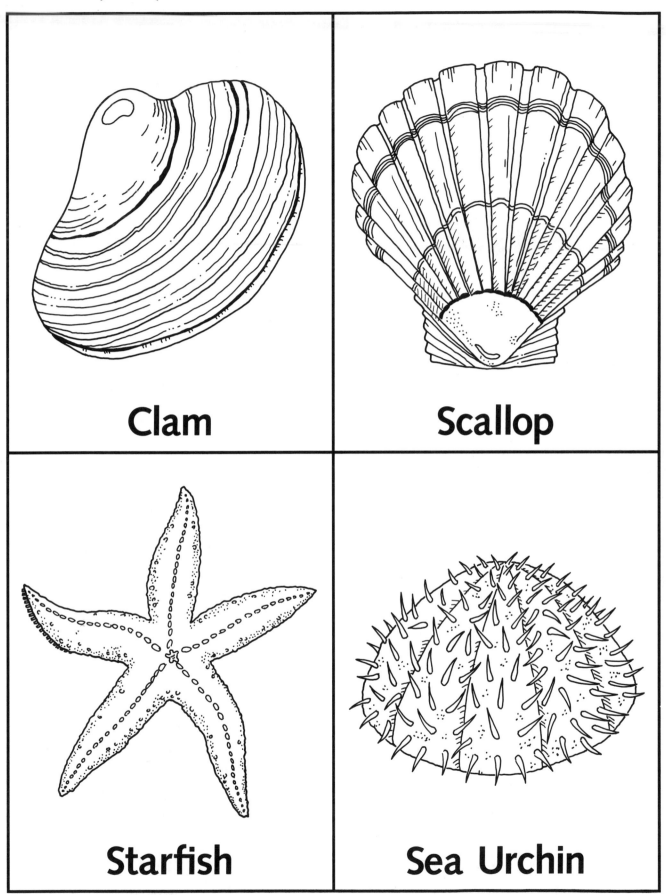

Clam

Scallop

Starfish

Sea Urchin

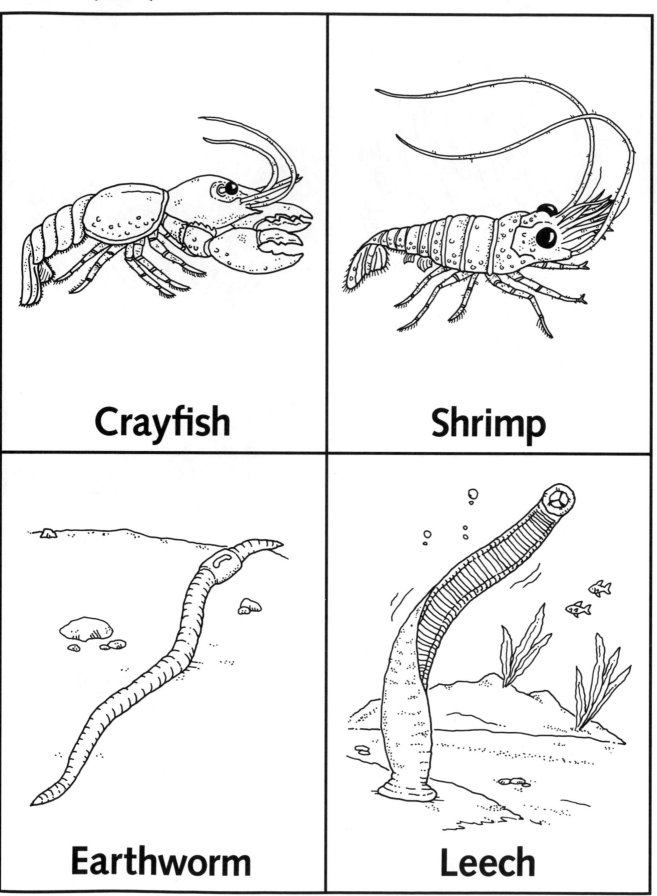

Crayfish

Shrimp

Earthworm

Leech

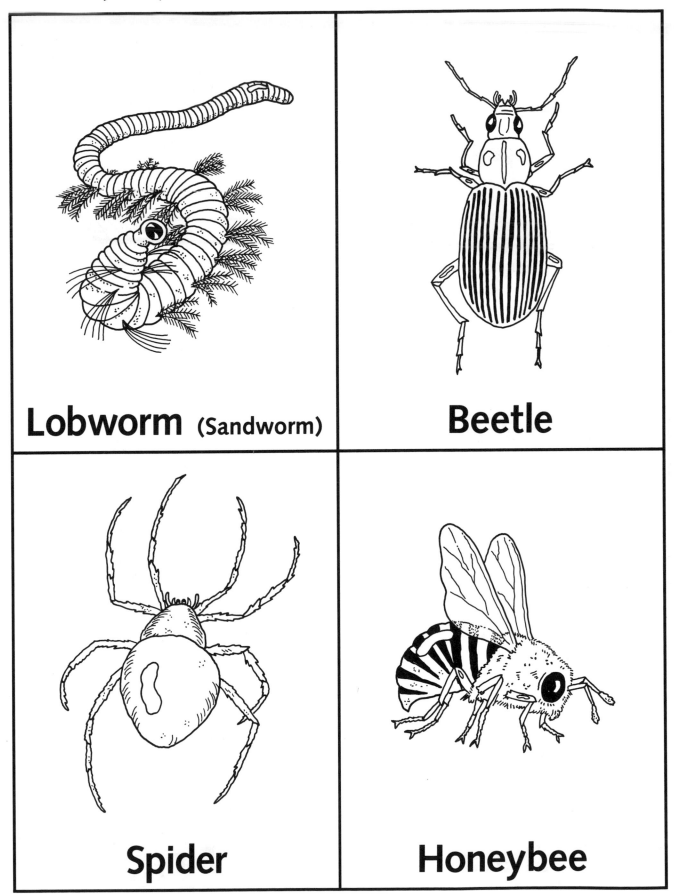

Lobworm (Sandworm)

Beetle

Spider

Honeybee

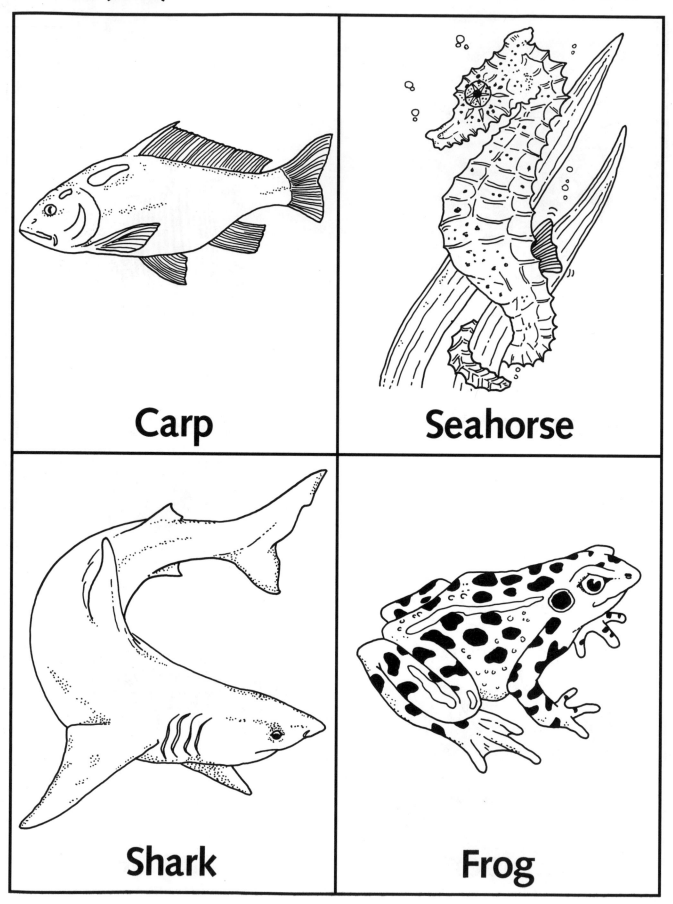

Carp

Seahorse

Shark

Frog

Newt and/or Salamander

Toad

Snake

Turtle

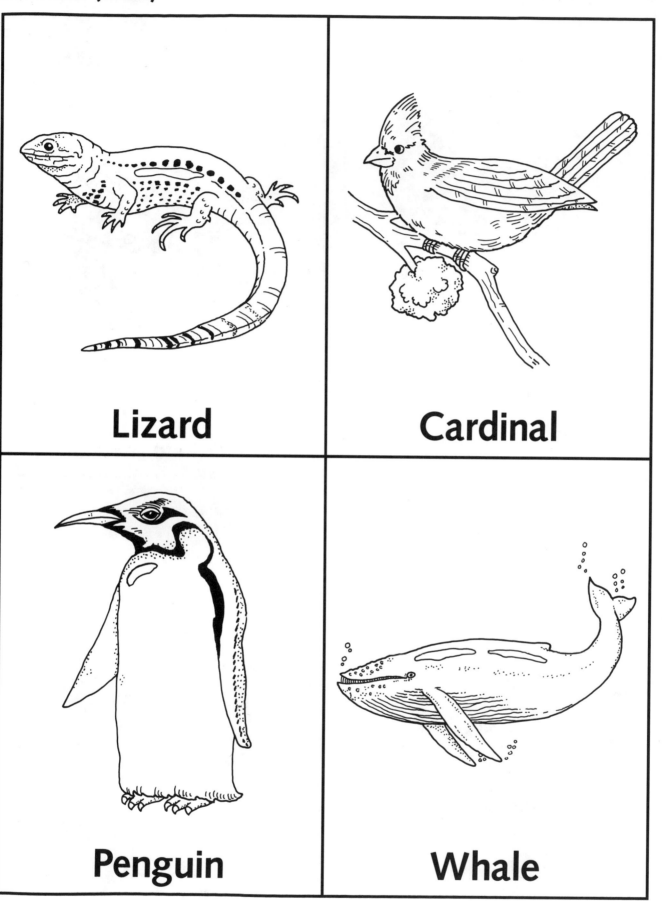

Lizard

Cardinal

Penguin

Whale

Elephant

Vole (Field Mouse)

Human

Paramecium & Ameba

What Newton Knew (Before Bike Helmets!)

Your students will put on their bicycle helmets and buckle their seatbelts more willingly after this 40-minute lesson when they realize these . . .

Science Concepts

1. Forces act on matter and cause motion.
2. An object in motion or at rest will remain in that state unless acted upon by another force. (This is Newton's First Law of Motion, otherwise known as the Law of Inertia.)

? Why Teach This?

Why the Earth keeps rotating and revolving, why people without seatbelts travel through windshields, and why children who don't wear bicycle helmets can suffer severe head injuries when they fall off their bikes can all be explained by the Law of Inertia.

It is easier to convince children to protect themselves if they understand the science concept behind the reminders to "buckle up."

You may also use this lesson to briefly review the Earth's motions of revolution and rotation, and their effects.

This lesson is vital in helping children understand that a mere handful of basic science concepts can explain many of the phenomena we experience in our everyday lives.

Cooperative Group Management

The children may work in either pairs or groups of four. Each child should have an opportunity to use the cup and ball for the demonstration and to observe what the ball does at all times.

Partner sharing and small group sharing along with representative participation will aid in completing the *Aha!* section, where the science concept is connected to real life.

Materials Needed

For each group
1. A small clear cylinder-shaped plastic or glass container. (Some 35mm film cases are now clear, and are perfect for this activity.)
2. A marble or small ball which fits into the container.

For each child
3. Data sheet.

✓ Getting Started

1. To relate this lesson to the previous lessons about animal adaptations, ask the children to brainstorm what a human's most valuable adaptation is. (The brain.)
2. Take a class survey to see who wears seatbelts in a car, and who wears a bicycle helmet.
3. Admit that you seem to be changing the subject entirely, but ask: Why does the Earth keep spinning (rotating) and moving about the sun (revolving)? Why doesn't it stop? What would happen if it did stop?
4. Explain that each child will have a chance to perform the demon-

stration and observe it while working with the cooperative group.

1 2 3 Procedure

1. Allow the students time to complete their hypotheses. (Encourage the children to answer part of the question, even if they don't feel able to answer all.)

   If the children choose to write about the Earth stopping its motion, acknowledge any hypotheses that state day and night would no longer alternate and the seasons would stop changing. But be sure to let the children know that something else would happen as well. They can discover this during the following activity.

2. The children should place the container on its side on the work surface. They should place the marble or ball midway into the container.

3. The demonstrating child should slide the container forward at a moderate speed, while everyone observes the motion of the ball. (The ball will appear to move backward into the container as the container moves forward. In reality, the ball will attempt to stay where it is, which can be explained by Newton's First Law of Motion, or inertia.)

4. When the container stops its forward motion, the children should observe that the ball continues to move forward, for the same reason explained in step 3. (Inertia.)

5. Have the groups repeat the activity several times before they write the observations.

6. Encourage small group discussion for the completion of the conclusion. Answers: not move or stay still, moves or acts on it, will keep moving, force.

7. The *Aha!* section should help the children realize why seatbelts and bike helmets are valuable in case of a sudden stop, and to understand what would happen to most objects on Earth's surface (including people) if the Earth suddenly stopped moving. Answers: 1. seatbelts, move forward; 2. stops suddenly, go head first onto the pavement.

8. Repeat the seatbelt and helmet surveys the next week to see if compliance has risen.

Connections

- **Consumer Science:** Have the children create safety posters or commercials about seatbelts and bike helmets.

- **Language Arts:** Have each small group do research about Sir Isaac Newton in a manner they choose and present findings.

- **Physics:** Have the children keep a "Newtonian Diary" for a week to observe everyday examples of the First Law. For instance, how does inertia affect forgotten homework, or new skaters trying to stop without using the force of gravity or a collision with a wall?

- **Reading:**
  Making Things Move, Neil Ardley. Watts, New York, 1984 (3–5).

  Why Doesn't the Earth Fall Up? and Other Not Such Dumb Questions About Motion, Vicki Cobb. Dutton, New York, 1988 (2–4).

  Movement, Brenda Walpole. Watts, New York, 1987 (3–6).

Physicist _____

What Newton Knew: Before Bike Helmets!

▲ **PROBLEM:** What would happen to riders if a car or a bike stopped its motion suddenly?

■ **HYPOTHESIS:** _____

_____

● **METHOD:**

1. Place the cup on its side. Place the marble or ball in the middle of it. Note the position of the ball both before and while you slide the cup forward at a moderate speed.

2. Suddenly, stop moving the cup. What happens to the ball?

👁 **OBSERVATIONS:**

1. At first the ball _____ When the cup moved, the

   marble _____

   _____

2. _____

   _____

★ **CONCLUSION:** Any object will _____

until a force _____ This is called *inertia*.

AHA!

1. *If a car stops suddenly, _____ are necessary to keep*

   passengers from continuing to _____ .

2. *A bike helmet helps protect my head, if my bike _____*

   and I _____ .

Rolling Into Physics

An energetic 40-minute session of rolling marbles will roll your physicists into these . . .

 **Science Concepts**

1. Energy can be transmitted through matter.
2. Inertia is a property of all objects. An object with more matter possesses more inertia, so it will require a greater amount of force (energy) to move it or to stop it moving.
3. When matter is moving, it is said to possess kinetic energy.
4. Energy is never lost, but it can leave a system and can change form (for example, from potential to kinetic energy).

 Why Teach This?

Understanding the above science concepts will help your students be more aware of energy changes all around them.

The reasons for safety procedures on playground equipment will become scientifically evident, and this lesson may even help your students become better defensive drivers when they grow up!

 Cooperative Group Management

The children should work in teams of two for the manipulation of the materials, but should compare their results within larger groups of four. Representative Sharing can be used for checking the conclusion.

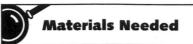 **Materials Needed**

For each group
1. A 12-in. or 30-cm ruler with a groove in the top surface so a marble can roll along it. If not available, substitute:
   a. An index card (3 × 5-in. size is sufficient).
   b. Scissors.
2. Any 30-cm ruler.
3. Five marbles of the same size and mass.
4. A larger, heavier marble. (Try to get a steel one from your local high school physics lab.)

For each child
Data sheet.

 **Getting Started**

1. Review Newton's First Law of Motion by asking for a few examples from real life. (See the previous lesson.)
2. Ask if anyone has ever pushed a large friend on a swing.
   Why is it so difficult to get the swing moving? Would it be easier or more difficult to get it moving if the swing had a very small child on it? Why? (The children should be able to infer from real life experience that the larger child possesses more inertia.)
3. Elicit why swing pushers get tired. (They are using up energy.) Where is the energy going? (It is being transferred to the swinger.)
4. What would happen if a child walked in front of a moving swing with a large child on it?

What would happen to the walker if a smaller child was on the swing?

 **Procedure**

1. Allow time for group discussion of the data sheet problems before the children write their hypothesis.

2. Explain that today the children are going bowling with marbles to discover if their hypotheses are correct.

   If you have grooved rulers, they will be the bowling alleys. If not, have the children construct a bowling alley by cutting a strip of index card 5 inches long and wide enough allow a 1 cm high wall on each side of a marble. Mark off centimeter increments along the track.

3. Discuss the fact that the children will have to carefully control the variable of muscle strength. To make the experiment as fair as possibe, they must try very hard to use the same amount of force to get each marble or set of marbles rolling.

4. Each partner should have the opportunity to use the marbles as required in the Method section, and to act as co-observer and measurer of how far the "bowling balls" at the end of the alley rolled. Be sure larger "ball" can roll without contacting the walls of the "alley."

5. Conclusion answers: 1. Kinetic or movement, can, other; 2. more kinetic or movement, pass or transfer; 3. bigger or more massive marble.

6. *Aha!* answers: 1. inertia or potential or kinetic energy, damage; 2. stay away, kinetic, injury.

 **Connections**

- **Independent Experimenting:** Allow time for the children to brainstorm the design of their own marble experiments. One idea to follow up on might be the effect of gravity on a marble's potential energy. What would happen if the marble rolled down a tilted ruler into other marbles? What if the angle of tilt was increased or decreased?

  Encourage the children to write up their experiments and prove their conclusion with measurement.

- **Physics:** See the lesson Play-ground Physics in *Dirt Cheap Science*.

- **Sports:** Have the children read the sports pages of the paper or sport magazines to clip and write captions explaining the energy changes and transfers taking place.

  For example, under a photo of a batter hitting a ball children might write: The player's energy came from solar energy. This changed into food (chemical) energy and muscular kinetic energy and finally into the kinetic energy of a hit!

- **Reading:**
  Making Things Move, Neil Ardley. Watts, New York, 1984 (3–5).

  Why Doesn't the Earth Fall Up? and Other Not Such Dumb Questions About Motion, Vicki Cobb. Dutton, New York, 1988 (2–4).

  Movement, Brenda Walpole. Watts, New York, 1987 (3–6).

  Forces in Action, Kathryn Whyman. Gloucester, New York, 1986 (3–6).

Rolling Into Physics

▲ PROBLEMS:

1. Can kinetic (movement) energy travel through objects and be transferred to other objects?

2. Will a more massive (heavier) object have more kinetic energy to pass along? Why do you think so?

■ HYPOTHESIS: _____

_____

● METHOD:

1. Place three marbles on the track at one end. Roll one marble of equal size toward them. What happens to the marbles? Measure any changes in position.

2. Using the same amount of muscular force, roll the more massive marble towards the three marbles placed at the track end. What happens to the marbles? Measure any changes in position.

3. Using the same amount of muscular force, roll two equally sized marbles against the three.
   What happens? Measure any changes.

☞ OBSERVATIONS:

1. _____

_____

_____

2. _____

_____

_____

3. _____

_____

_____

★ CONCLUSION:

1. _____ energy _____ travel through objects, to be transferred to _____ objects.

2. Objects with more mass also have _____ energy to _____ along.

3. When two marbles rolled into the other marbles, the results were more like those with the _____ than with one marble.

AHA!

1. *Cars are safer on roads without large trucks because trucks have more* _____. *Trucks are more likely to* _____ *cars in a collision between the two.*

2. *Good playground behavior means that children should* _____ _____ *from moving equipment to avoid an unwanted transfer of* _____ *energy which could cause* _____

_____.

The Great Domino Derby!

The ultimate in a series of two or three cooperative learning sessions combines domino dynamics with fun, patience, and planning with partners. It will help your engineers master these . . .

Science Concepts

1. An event's properties are determined by objects, the space they occupy, and the time which passes during the event.
2. The interaction of matter and energy can change the form of the energy and the position of the matter. A group of interacting objects and energy changes is called a system.
3. Energy may exist within an object as potential energy (depending on its position) or as kinetic energy (if it is in motion).
4. Energy entering a system may be transferred within that system through a series of interactions, and finally exit the system.

 ## Why Teach This?

This is a wonderfully rewarding activity for groups that have mastered the art of cooperative behavior. It will also provide inspiration and motivation for groups that have had trouble with their cooperative skills.

Expect screams of joy and frustration as the children test and try to improve upon their derby designs. Troubleshooting and "going back to the drawing board" are valid learning experiences which your students will hopefully internalize for life.

By discovering how changing one part of a system will affect other parts in ways that may not be foreseen, children receive a powerful object lesson that applies to all systems, including ecosystems and the human body. If they understand this principle, they may think twice before disrupting those systems with pollution or drugs.

Cooperative Group Management

I do not recommend giving this lesson until your children have been accustomed to working within cooperative groups for at least several months.

The lesson is best handled in groups of four working with one set of dominoes. The cooperative methods of partner sharing and group sharing work particularly well if the group divides the dominoes into two piles. Partners can share their ideas, try them out, and then incorporate them with the ideas from the other half of the team.

Each team should practice constructive criticism and positive comments as well.

Accidents with dominoes are sure to occur, so be prepared to deal with frustration. Encourage brainstorming of how to avoid further problems. For example, long sweatshirt sleeves pose hazards to domino systems.

One of my students came up with a wonderful method of keeping the domino system from running prematurely. He and his team analyzed the system to find key dominoes to keep out of the design until they were ready to run it.

Each group will need a timer. If you wish, each group may also have a secretary to draw up a final set of plans which can be replicated by another group.

Materials Needed

1. A clock with a second hand.
2. (*optional*) A video recorder. (The children will love seeing their systems played on tape. Pre-derby interviews about predictions and post-run troubleshooting comments make wonderful models for future classes, and for showing parents the excitement generated in your "hands-on" science classes!)

For each group
3. A box of 55 dominoes. (Ask for class donations, or purchase them from a toy store at about $2 each.)
4. Four marbles.
5. Found objects which can be integrated into the systems, e.g.: 30 ml measuring cups, small blocks to build "domino staircases," etc.
6. A ruler (for accurate placement of dominoes and found objects).
7. Several index cards (to make tracks for marble runs).
8. Scissors.

For each student
9. Data sheet.

Getting Started

1. Ask the children to review their conclusions from Rolling Into Physics (page 101) and then allow time for the groups to complete the review questions at the top of the data sheet. Answers: 1. system; 2. potential; 3. kinetic.

2. Draw the children's attention to the small diagram of a domino system and the legend explaining the objects in it. Allow time for the children to analyze the diagram with their group, call upon a representative to explain how it might work, and get group estimates of how long the children think the system will take to run. (Expect outlandish predictions in minutes rather than seconds. This lesson will also teach your students that a lot can occur in a very short period of time.)

The diagram shows dominoes in a serpentine line passing their kinetic energy into a marble, which must run along a track to move another set of dominoes which move another marble which finally rolls off the table into a cup. Explain that the arrows serve as vectors to explain the direction of the force or energy being used.

Be sure to discuss the fact that energy must be placed into the system from their body's energy. Also discuss the fact that although the energy leaves the system when the last domino or marble falls, it is not lost. Ask what happens to it. (The energy will have entered into the floor or table, causing its molecules to vibrate as sound and heat energy.)

Procedure

1. Explain that each child is responsible for generating a plan using 27 or fewer dominoes, along with any other objects, if desired. The child is to sketch the plan upon the data sheet and then share it with a partner. They should assess each other's designs and take turns trying them out. (You may wish to assign the initial design as a homework activity.)

2. Before trying out each design, the children should write a time prediction. They should then note the actual time taken. They should run several repetitions and timings of the final partner plan.

3. Because this activity will take place over several sessions, emphasize that the children should continually update their diagrams to record improvements and avoid repeating mistakes. (Point out that scientists always take good notes to help them remember and chart their progress.)

   A written analysis of the system's weaknesses and strengths offers a unique homework assignment.

4. When the partners are relatively satisfied with their own plan, they should examine the plan of the other partners in their team. All four should study how to combine the two designs into a system which utilizes all the dominoes and any other objects incorporated into the designs.

5. The group should make a time prediction for the final Domino Derby. At this stage the prediction should be fairly accurate. (The children will be fascinated to see if the running times of the two mini-systems add up to the running time of the final design.)

6. Be sure to allow time for each group to demonstrate its system to the rest of the class, either live or on tape.

7. Some groups may wish to combine their domino systems with other groups to make "supersystems." This calls for tremendous cooperation, and pays off with tremendous enthusiasm and excitement!

 **Connections**

- **Word Analysis:** Discuss what the "domino effect" means. Challenge the children to find examples of this "effect," in which one change causes a series of others.

- **Ecology:** See All About Changes: A Succession Hunt (page 47) so the children can apply the "domino theory" to nature.

- **Biography:** Have the children investigate Rube Goldberg and his fascinating systems for accomplishing so little while utilizing so much.

- **Technology:** Challenge the children to build their own Rube Goldberg system to accomplish something they dislike doing—like taking out the garbage or clearing the table. They can draw detailed diagrams and also write statements to explain what energy changes are taking place.

- **Math:** Have the children calculate the total distance that energy travels through their domino system, and compare it to the distances of the other systems. They might also calculate the speed by dividing the distance by the number of seconds the system takes to run.

- **Reading:**
Making Things Move, Neil Ardley. Watts, New York, 1984 (3–5).

Why Doesn't the Earth Fall Up? and Other Not Such Dumb Questions About Motion, Vicki Cobb. Dutton, New York, 1988 (2–4).

Movement, Brenda Walpole. Watts, New York, 1987 (3–6).

Forces in Action, Kathryn Whyman. Gloucester, New York, 1986 (3–6).

Domino Derby

1. A group of interacting objects in a bike, human body, or nature

   is called a _____.

2. A domino which is standing has the potential to change

   position, so it has _____ energy.

3. When the domino moves, it has _____ energy.

4. Analyze the diagram and discuss how it might work as a
   system. Estimate how long it will take for the energy to pass
   through.

Legend: 🁢 = domino   ● = marble   ▭ = track   → = direction
                                                          of force   _____
                                                                              seconds

| Plan 1: | Using 27 dominoes, and other objects, design and draw by yourself. (Use the back of this paper to draw.) |

Time Prediction = _____ seconds   Actual Time = _____ seconds

| Plan 2: | With your partner, design, draw and test your plan. (27 dominoes & other objects) (Use the back of this paper to draw.) |

Time Prediction = _____ seconds   Actual Time = _____ seconds

| Plan 3: | Revised Partner Plan using 27 dominoes and other objects. (Use the back of this paper to draw.) |

Time Prediction = _____ seconds   Actual Time = _____ seconds

Work with the other members of your group to combine your
domino plans. Draw the plan, predict the time, set up
the plan, and run it.

Time Out Thinking

_____
Name

_____
Date

1. Why do you think you ended up at the Time Out Area?

   _____

2. What plan can you come up with to keep this from happening again?

   _____

   _____

3. Do you wish to speak to me privately about this? _____

4. Please have a parent sign this to indicate you have discussed this at home.

   _____
   Parent's Signature

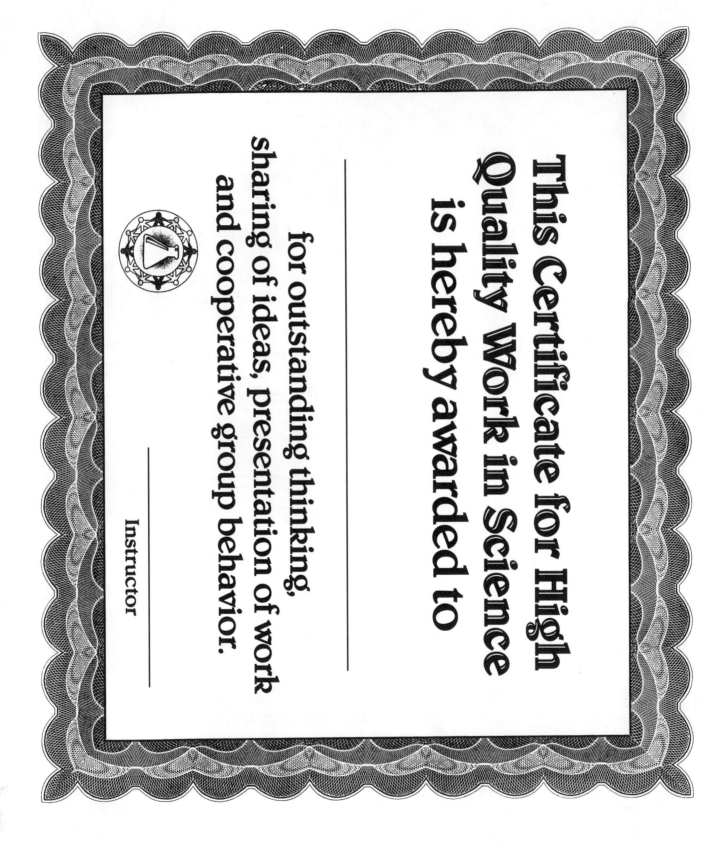

This Certificate for High Quality Work in Science

is hereby awarded to

_____

for outstanding thinking,
sharing of ideas, presentation of work
and cooperative group behavior.

_____
Instructor

Notes